Contents

www.harcourtschoolsupply.com
© Harcourt Achieve Inc. All rights reserved.

Introduction

The contents of this book are based upon the National Science Education Standards for Grade 2. These standards include (A) Unifying Concepts and Processes, (B) Science as Inquiry, (C) Physical Science, (D) Life Science, (E) Earth and Space Science, (F) Science and Technology, (G) Science in Personal and Social Perspectives, and (H) History and Nature of Science.

This book will help teachers, students, parents, and tutors. Teachers can use this book either to introduce or review a topic in their science classroom. Students will find the book useful in reviewing the major concepts in science. Parents can use this book to help their children with topics that may be posing a problem in the classroom. Tutors can use this book as a basis for their lessons and for assigning questions and activities.

This book includes nine lessons that focus on the nine major concepts presented in the content standards: Physical Science, Life Science, and Earth and Space Science. The lessons also cover the sixteen major concepts presented in the other standards. A table on page 4 provides a correlation between the contents of each lesson and the National Science Education Standards.

Before beginning the book, the reader can check his or her knowledge of the content by completing the *Assessment*. The *Assessment* consists of questions that deal with the content standards. This will allow the reader to determine how much he or she knows about a particular concept before beginning to read about it. The *Assessment* may also serve as a way of leading the reader to a specific lesson that may be of special interest.

Each lesson follows the same sequence in presenting the material. A list of *Key Terms* is always provided at the beginning of each lesson. This list includes all the boldfaced terms and their definitions presented in the same order that they are introduced in the lesson. The reader can develop a sense of the lesson content by glancing through the *Key Terms*. Each lesson then provides background information about the concept. This information is divided into several sections. Each section is written so that the reader is not overwhelmed with details. Rather, the reader is guided through the concept in a logical sequence. Each lesson then moves on to a *Review*. This section consists of several multiple-choice and short-answer questions. The multiple-choice questions check if the reader has retained information that was covered in the lesson. The short-answer questions

check if the reader can use information from the lesson to provide the answers.

Each lesson then moves on to a series of activities. These activities are designed to check the reader's understanding of the information. Some activities are an extension of the lesson by presenting additional information. The activities are varied so as not to be boring. For example, reading passages about interesting and unusual findings are included. Questions to check reading comprehension are then asked. As a change of pace, some activities are meant to engage the reader in a "fun-type" exercise. These activities include crosswords, word searches, jumbled letters, and cryptograms.

The last activity in each lesson is an experiment. Each experiment has been designed so that the required items are easy to locate and can usually be found in most households. Care has been taken to avoid the use of any dangerous materials or chemicals. However, an adult should always be present when a student is conducting an experiment. In some cases, the experimental procedure reminds students that adult supervision is required. Before beginning any experiment, an adult should review the list of materials and the procedure. In this way, the adult will be aware of any situations that may need special attention. The adult should review the safety issues before the experiment is begun. The adult may want to check a laboratory manual for specific safety precautions that should be followed when doing an experiment, such as wearing safety goggles and never touching or tasting chemicals.

The book then follows with a *Science Fair* section. Information is presented on how to conduct and present a science fair project. In some cases, the experiment at the end of a lesson can serve as the basis for a science fair project. Additional suggestions are also provided with advice as to how to choose an award-winning science fair project.

A *Glossary* is next. This section lists all the boldfaced terms in alphabetical order and indicates the page on which the term is used. The book concludes with an *Answer Key*, which gives the answers to all the activity questions, including the experiment.

This book has been designed and written so that teachers, students, parents, and tutors will find it easy to use and follow. Most importantly, students will benefit from this book by achieving at a higher level in class and on standardized tests.

www.harcourtschoolsupply.com
© Harcourt Achieve Inc. All rights reserved.

National Science Education Standards
Grades K-4

Standard A: UNIFYING CONCEPTS AND PROCESSES

A1 Systems, order, and organization
A2 Evidence, models, and explanation
A3 Change, constancy, and measurement
A4 Evolution and equilibrium
A5 Form and function

Standard B: SCIENCE AS INQUIRY

B1 Abilities necessary to do scientific inquiry
B2 Understanding about scientific inquiry

Standard C: PHYSICAL SCIENCE

C1 Properties of objects and materials
C2 Position and motion of objects
C3 Light, heat, electricity, and magnetism

Standard D: LIFE SCIENCE

D1 Characteristics of organisms
D2 Life cycles of organisms
D3 Organisms and environments

Standard E: EARTH AND SPACE SCIENCE

E1 Properties of earth materials
E2 Objects in the sky
E3 Changes in earth and sky

Standard F: SCIENCE AND TECHNOLOGY

F1 Abilities to distinguish between natural objects
    and objects made by humans
F2 Abilities of technological design
F3 Understanding about science and technology

Standard G: SCIENCE IN PERSONAL AND SOCIAL PERSPECTIVES

G1 Personal health
G2 Characteristics and changes in populations
G3 Types of resources
G4 Changes in environments
G5 Science and technology in local challenges

Standard H: HISTORY AND NATURE OF SCIENCE

H1 Science as a human endeavor

www.harcourtschoolsupply.com
© Harcourt Achieve Inc. All rights reserved.

Correlation to National Science Education Standards

Assessment

Darken the circle by the best answer.

Lesson 1

1. Which state of matter has a definite shape?
- (A) solid
- (B) liquid
- (C) gas

2. What can you find using a balance?
- (A) state
- (B) size
- (C) mass

Lesson 2

3. What is your distance when you run?
- (A) how fast you move
- (B) how far you go
- (C) where you go

4. What do you need to measure speed?
- (A) time and mass
- (B) mass and size
- (C) distance and time

Lesson 3

5. What is heat?
- (A) a state of matter
- (B) the moving of charge
- (C) the flow of energy

6. What do all magnets have in common?
- (A) They pull everything.
- (B) They have two poles.
- (C) They are long and thin.

Lesson 4

7. Where do plants get energy?
- (A) from soil
- (B) from sunlight
- (C) from animals

8. What are a puppy's cells?
- (A) the smallest units of its body
- (B) the places it lives
- (C) the food it eats

Lesson 5

9. What do all baby mammals have in common?
- (A) They start out in eggs.
- (B) They drink milk from their mothers.
- (C) They start out as seeds.

10. What happens in a cocoon?
- (A) A seed turns into a plant.
- (B) An animal grows in a pouch.
- (C) A caterpillar changes into a butterfly.

www.harcourtschoolsupply.com
© Harcourt Achieve Inc. All rights reserved.

Assessment, page 2

Lesson 6

11. Some animals are good at staying warm. In which environment would these animals most likely live?
- Ⓐ desert
- Ⓑ tundra
- Ⓒ rain forest

12. What passes along a food chain?
- Ⓐ soil
- Ⓑ plants
- Ⓒ energy

Lesson 7

13. Why are rocks a resource?
- Ⓐ They are hard.
- Ⓑ They can be sold.
- Ⓒ People can use them.

14. Which of these is for transportation?
- Ⓐ a boat in water
- Ⓑ a large rock on the ground
- Ⓒ a tall tree in the soil

Lesson 8

15. A glowing ball of gas in the sky is a
- Ⓐ moon.
- Ⓑ star.
- Ⓒ solar system.

16. Which sentence about the sun is true?
- Ⓐ The sun is the closest constellation.
- Ⓑ The sun is the closest planet.
- Ⓒ The sun is the closest star.

Lesson 9

17. How long does it take for Earth to orbit the sun?
- Ⓐ one hour
- Ⓑ one day
- Ⓒ one year

18. What causes day and night?
- Ⓐ Earth orbits the sun.
- Ⓑ Earth rotates on its axis.
- Ⓒ Earth tilts on its axis.

Lesson 1 Properties of Objects and Materials

It is a sunny day. You go outside to play. Maybe you throw a ball to a friend. Perhaps you jump rope or ride your bicycle.

Your toys are made of **matter**. All things are made of matter. Even you are made of matter. The picture shows matter at the playground.

Mass

All matter has mass. The **mass** of an object is the amount of matter it

matter—anything that has mass and takes up space

mass—the amount of matter in an object

property—a trait that can describe matter

texture—the way a sample of matter feels

solid—matter that has a certain shape and size

liquid—matter that has a certain size but takes the shape of its container

gas—matter that does not have a certain size or shape

balance—a tool that measures mass

volume—the amount of space an object takes up

has. Have you ever picked up a bowling ball? Have you ever picked up a tennis ball? There is more matter in the bowling ball. The mass of a bowling ball is greater than the mass of a tennis ball.

Space

All matter takes up space. Books are an example of matter. Your books take up space in your desk.

Some objects take up more space than others. Think about the bowling ball and the tennis ball. The bowling ball takes up more space than the tennis ball.

Properties

Matter has properties. A **property** is a trait or characteristic. Mass is a property. The amount of space an object takes up is another property.

Color and shape are other properties. So are smell and texture. **Texture** is how an object feels.

What properties describe an apple? You might say that an apple is <u>round</u> and <u>red</u>. The outside of an apple is <u>smooth</u>. An apple tastes <u>sweet</u>. These words describe the properties of an apple.

Apple

Shape:	round
Color:	red
Texture:	smooth
Taste:	sweet

Forms of Matter

Think about looking up into the sky. You might see a bird flying through the air. You might see rain falling. The bird, air, and rain are all matter. They are very different.

Matter has three different forms. It can be a solid, a liquid, or a gas.

Solids A key is solid matter. A **solid** is matter that has a shape that does not change. The key can be on a keychain. A key can

be in a pocket. Wherever the key is, its shape stays the same.

The amount of space a solid takes up also stays the same. The size of the key does not change. The key does not get bigger or smaller.

Each solid has its own size and shape. These properties do not change unless you cut, bend, or break the object.

Can you find solids around you? Your desk and chair are solids. Your books and pencil are solids.

Liquids Rain is liquid matter. **Liquid** matter has mass. It also takes up space.

A liquid does not have a certain shape. It changes shape depending on where it is. A drop of water looks like a raindrop in the air. It flattens out when it hits the ground.

A liquid flows. It takes the shape of its container. The picture shows what happens when you pour water into different containers. The amount of liquid stays the same. Its shape changes.

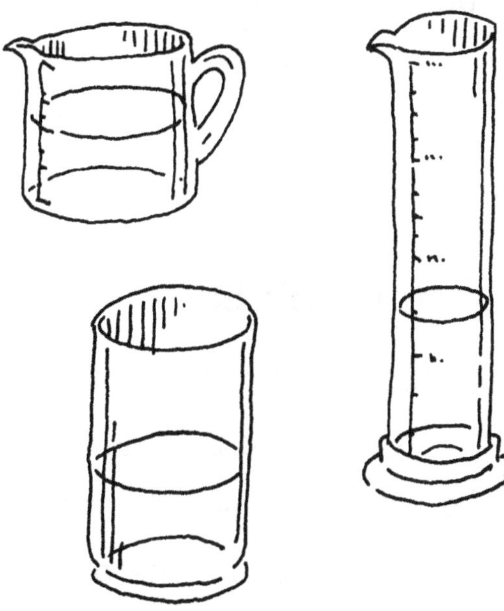

Gases Air is a gas. Like other forms of matter, a **gas** has mass and takes up space. Like a liquid, a gas does not have a certain shape.

A gas is different from a solid or a liquid. A gas is the only form of matter that does not take up a certain amount of space. A gas fills all the space in its container.

www.harcourtschoolsupply.com
© Harcourt Achieve Inc. All rights reserved.

If you add a small amount of a gas to a room, it spreads out. It can fill the entire room. That same amount of gas can be squeezed into a small container.

You can't see many gases because they do not have color. Air is all around you. You cannot see it. You know it is there because you breathe it in. You also know it is there because air can lift a kite, fill a balloon, or blow a bubble.

Measuring Solids

You can measure the mass of a solid. You use a tool called a **balance**. Place the solid on one side of the balance. Put masses on the other side until the two sides are even. Add the numbers shown on the masses. The total is the mass of the solid.

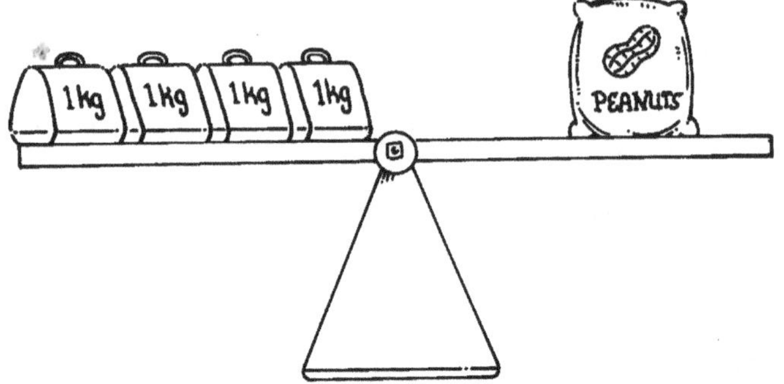

You can measure how big a solid is. You can find the length of a solid. You can also find how wide a solid is. You use a ruler.

A tape measure is like a ruler. It bends around objects. You can use a tape measure to find how big around a solid is.

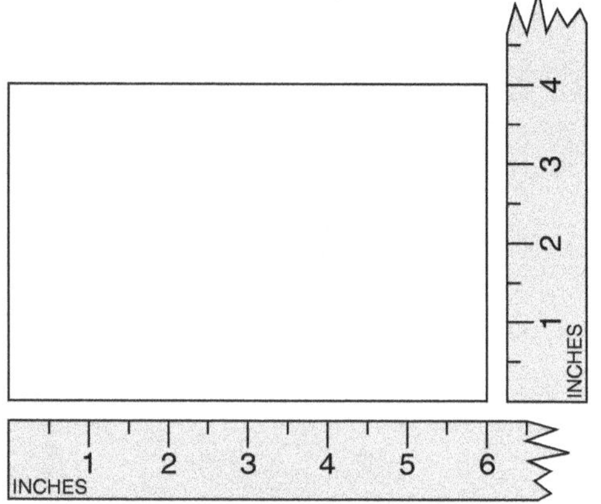

Measuring Liquids

You can measure the mass of a liquid. It is like finding the mass of a solid. The difference is that you cannot pour a liquid onto a balance.

Start by finding the mass of an empty container. Then add the liquid to it. Find the mass of the container with the liquid. The change is the mass of the liquid.

www.harcourtschoolsupply.com
© Harcourt Achieve Inc. All rights reserved.

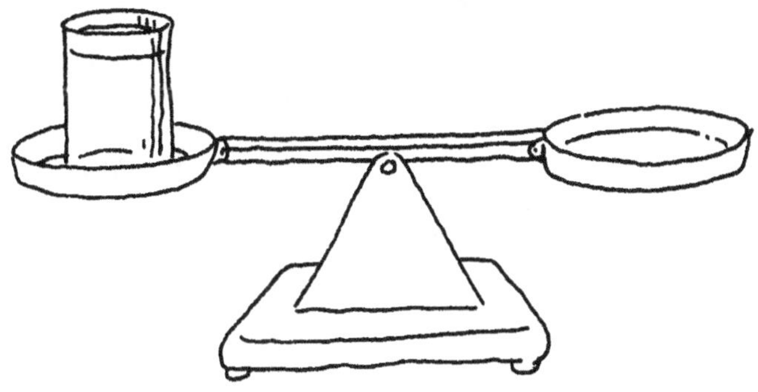

Have you ever measured water in a measuring cup? If so, you have found the volume of the water. The **volume** of a liquid is the amount of space it takes up. A milliliter is a unit used to measure the volume of a liquid.

Measuring Gases

Do you feel air above you? You probably do not. This makes it hard to believe that air has mass, but it does. The mass of a balloon filled with air is greater than the mass of an empty balloon.

www.harcourtschoolsupply.com
© Harcourt Achieve Inc. All rights reserved.

Lesson 1   Review

Darken the circle by the best answer.

1. Color is one of an elephant's

  Ⓐ masses.

  Ⓑ volumes.

  Ⓒ properties.

2. What do you know about an object if you know its mass?

  Ⓐ where it is located

  Ⓑ what it feels like

  Ⓒ how much matter it has

3. Which of these objects takes up the most space?

  Ⓐ marble

  Ⓑ skateboard

  Ⓒ fingernail

4. Which of these is a solid?

  Ⓐ apple

  Ⓑ air

  Ⓒ juice

5. Unlike a solid, a liquid

  Ⓐ has mass.

  Ⓑ matches the shape of its container.

  Ⓒ keeps the same shape and size.

6. Which of these tools can you use to measure the mass of a book?

  Ⓐ tape measure

  Ⓑ ruler

  Ⓒ balance

7. What are two properties of all types of matter?

____

____

____

____

Lesson 1   All About Matter

Circle each term listed below in the puzzle.

balance	mass	solid
gas	matter	texture
liquid	property	volume

```
V T E X T U R E R I H L
O N B C H D R Y M A S S
I G A S A O I E H J T T
X V O L U M E N P G K T
P Y A E F K L F R T B G
I G R D Y R I X O H A I
S O L I D M Q X P A L G
Y F E J U W U O E S A B
S C S L B U I H R A N X
D Z O S R J D V T N C T
M A T T E R G E Y N E L
N C P A O D B W M N X N
```


www.harcourtschoolsupply.com
© Harcourt Achieve Inc. All rights reserved.

Lesson 1 — Solids, Liquids, and Gases

Fill in key terms that complete each sentence. Choose from the words below.

balance	mass	solid
gas	matter	texture
liquid	property	volume

1. Any sample of _____________ has mass and takes up space.

2. Sandpaper has a rough _____________.

3. A baseball is a _____________ because it has a certain shape and size.

4. The _____________ of an object is the amount of matter in it.

5. A _____________ is a trait that describes matter.

6. You can use a _____________ to measure the mass of a stone.

7. Milk is a _____________ because its shape changes to match its container.

8. The _____________ of a liquid tells how much space it takes up.

9. Air is a _____________ that takes the size and shape of the balloon.

Lesson 1   States of Matter

**Look at the pictures. Write <u>solid</u>, <u>liquid</u>, or <u>gas</u> on the line beside
each picture.**

1.    ____

2.    ____

3.    ____

4.    ____

5. ____

www.harcourtschoolsupply.com
© Harcourt Achieve Inc. All rights reserved.

Lesson 1, States of Matter
Science 2, SV 9781419034305

Lesson 1 Properties of Matter

The pictures show different types of matter. On the lines, write at least two properties of each object in the picture. The first one has been done for you.

1. 

hard   big

2. 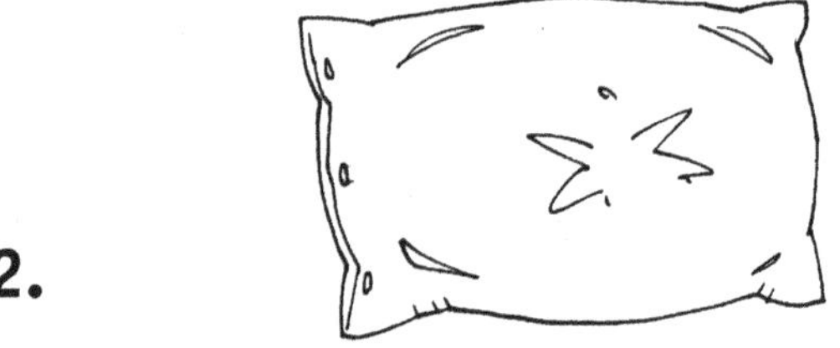

_______________   _______________

3. 

_______________   _______________

4. 

_______________   _______________

www.harcourtschoolsupply.com
© Harcourt Achieve Inc. All rights reserved.

Lesson 1   Changing States of Water

During a winter storm, water might freeze into ice. Ice is solid water. Ice can form when the temperature is 0°C or lower.

When the storm ends, ice can melt. When ice melts, it changes from a solid to a liquid. This happens when the temperature goes above 0°C.

The sun might heat a puddle of liquid water. This can make the liquid water evaporate. When water evaporates, it changes into water vapor. You cannot see water vapor. It is in the air around you.

Draw a picture showing how water can change into different states.

© Harcourt Achieve Inc. All rights reserved.

Lesson 1 — Experiment: Investigating the Mass of a Gas

It can be hard to believe that air has mass. After all, you do not feel it. In this experiment, you will prove that air has mass.

What You Will Need

2 balloons

2 straws

tape

ruler

black marker

Procedure

1. Fill one balloon with air and tie the opening closed.

2. Tape the straws together. Make a mark at the middle point.

3. Place your finger under the mark on the straw. Balance the straw on your finger.

4. Tape the filled balloon to one end of the straws.

5. Tape the empty balloon to the other end of the straws.

6. Place your finger under the mark on the straw.

7. Try to balance the straw on your finger. Observe if the straw becomes balanced. If not, look at which balloon is lower than the other.

Experiment: Investigating the Mass of a Gas (cont'd.)

Analysis

1. Why did you balance the straw on your finger without the balloons?

\
\
\
\

2. Were you able to balance the straw with the balloons taped on it?

\
\
\
\

Conclusion

Based on your observations, does air have mass? Explain your answer.

\
\
\
\

Lesson 2   Position and Motion of Objects

How do you get from one place to another? You move! You might walk or run. You might ride a bicycle or skateboard. You might even ride in a car or bus.

All of these examples involve a change in position. Your **position** is the place where you are located.

How would you describe your position right now? Are you sitting at your desk? Maybe you are in the library or at home. All objects can be described by their position. The children in the picture are playing in different positions.

Motion

An object is in **motion** if its position changes. As you walk from one place to another, you are in motion. A ball is in motion as it rolls across a field. A bus is in motion as it drives down the street. Can you think of other examples of motion?

Key Terms

position—the location of an object

motion—a change in the position of an object

distance—the length an object moves

speed—how fast or slowly an object moves

You can measure how far a person or an object moves. This length is known as **distance**. To measure distance, you can use a ruler or a tape measure.

Distance is measured in units of length. A common unit of length is the meter. To give you an idea how long a meter is, look at a doorknob. Most doorknobs are about one meter above the floor.

Distance

Suppose a friend asks you to move over so she can pass by. When this happens, you move just a little bit. Suppose you walk down the street to a friend's house. This time you move a lot farther.

Speed

On your mark, get set, go! The swimmers dive into a pool. They race to the other end as fast as they can. The person who swims the fastest wins the race.

www.harcourtschoolsupply.com
© Harcourt Achieve Inc. All rights reserved.

Lesson 2, Position and Motion of Objects
Science 2, SV 9781419034305

You can measure how fast or how slowly a person or an object moves. This measure is called **speed**.

To measure speed, you need to know how far an object moves. You also need to know how long it takes to move. A faster swimmer can reach the end of the pool in a shorter amount of time. A slower swimmer takes longer to move the same distance.

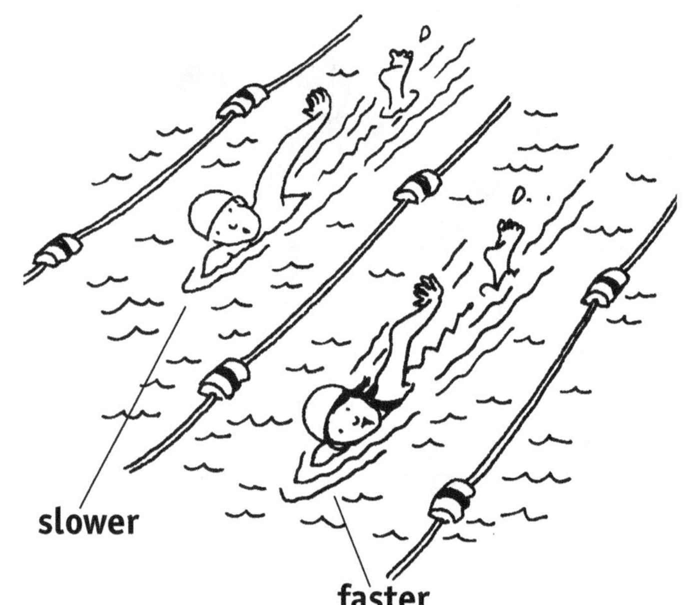

www.harcourtschoolsupply.com
© Harcourt Achieve Inc. All rights reserved.

Lesson 2, Position and Motion of Objects
Science 2, SV 9781419034305

Lesson 2   Review

Darken the circle by the best answer.

1. What does the position of an object describe?

   (A) how far it has moved

   (B) where it is located

   (C) how fast it is moving

2. What changes about an object when it is in motion?

   (A) its position

   (B) its shape

   (C) its size

3. What type of tool might you use to measure distance?

   (A) stopwatch

   (B) measuring cup

   (C) ruler

4. Which measurement describes how fast an object moves?

   (A) mass

   (B) speed

   (C) distance

5. What does it mean to say that a car is in motion?

____

____

____

6. How are distance and time related to speed?

____

____

____

www.harcourtschoolsupply.com
© Harcourt Achieve Inc. All rights reserved.

Lesson 2   **Position**

There are different ways to describe the position of an object. On the lines below, write one way to describe the position of each shape.

Try to use some of the following words in your descriptions.

under	next to	on top of	above
to the left of	to the right of	between	

An example is done for you.

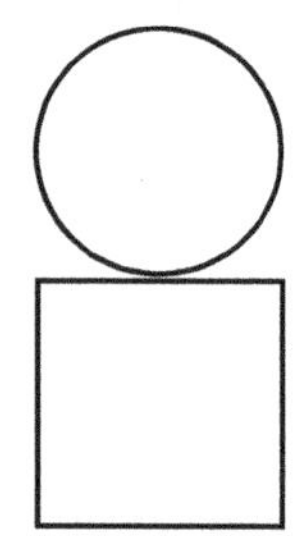 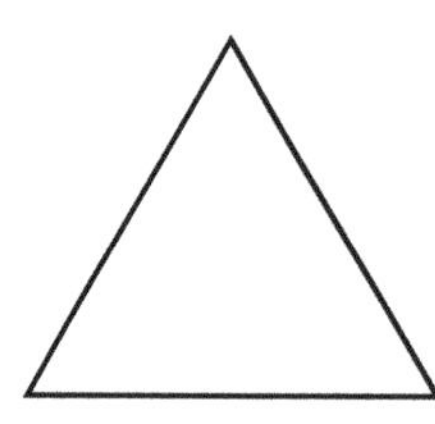 

Sample: The square is under the circle.

Circle: ____

____

Square: ____

____

Triangle: ____

____

Star: ____

____

Lesson 2   **Showing Motion**

Draw a picture of an object in motion. It might even be you. Write <u>START</u> at the starting position. Write <u>END</u> at the ending position.

© Harcourt Achieve Inc. All rights reserved.

Lesson 2   Distance

A ruler has numbers on it. The numbers tell how long something is. Many rulers have two sets of numbers. One side measures in inch units. The other side measures in centimeter units. Scientists usually measure things using centimeters.

Use a centimeter ruler. Measure the distance each bee flies.

1. 

2. 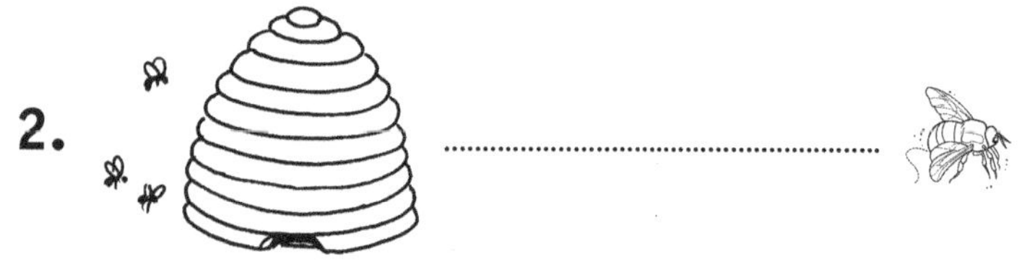

3. 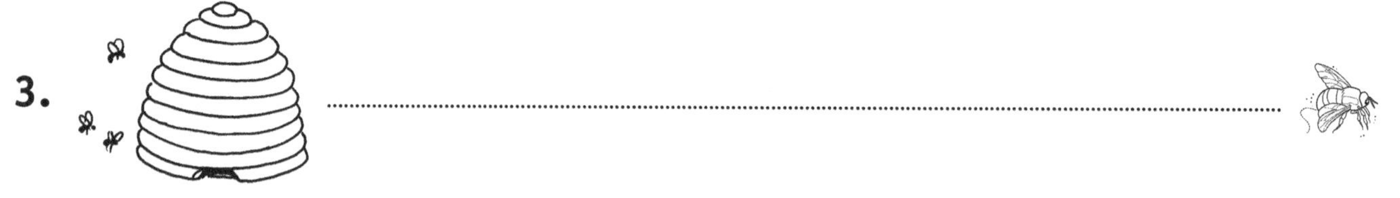

4. 

www.harcourtschoolsupply.com
© Harcourt Achieve Inc. All rights reserved.

Lesson 2   Speed

Look at the pictures of moving things. Put the objects in order of how fast you think they move.

Write the numbers 1 through 5 on the lines to show the order. Write <u>1</u> under the slowest object. Write <u>5</u> under the fastest object. Fill in the numbers for the objects in between.

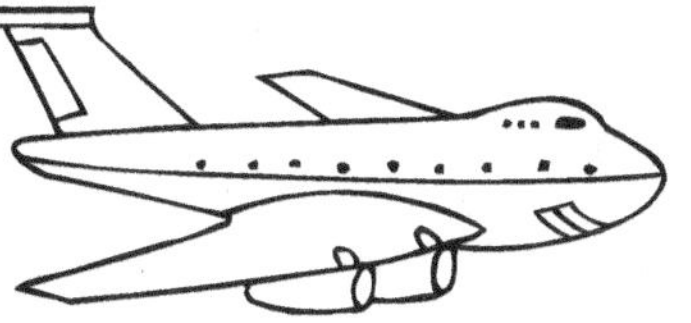

____

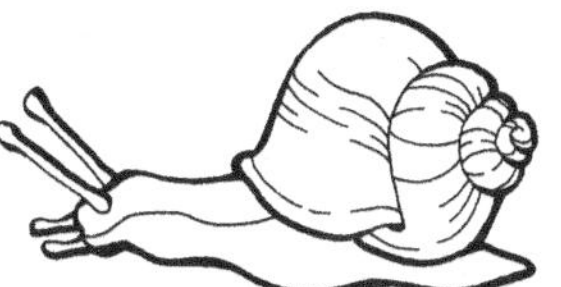

____

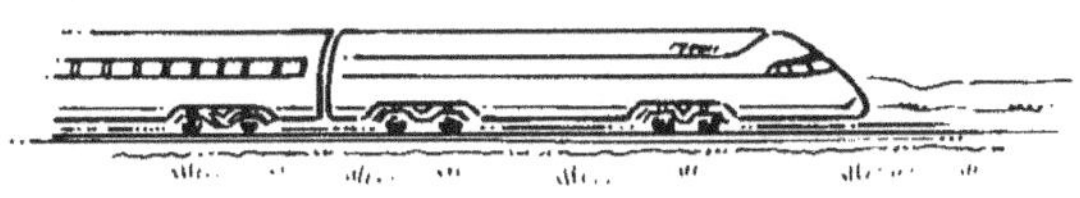

____

____

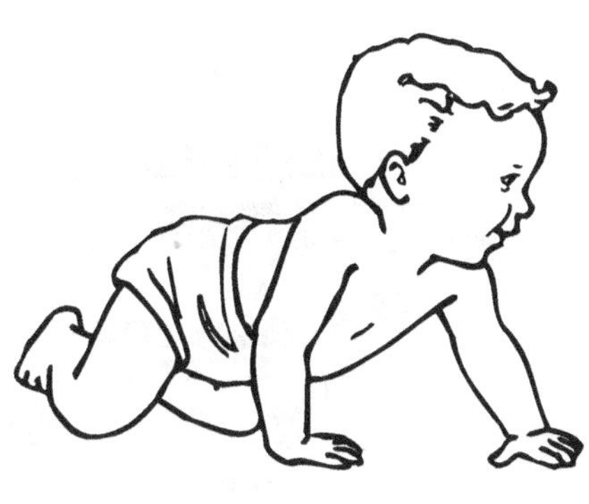

____

Lesson 2   The Crawler

Read the following passage. Then answer the questions that follow the passage.

What comes to mind when you think about the space shuttle? Do you picture a rocket zooming through the air? Or maybe you imagine a rocket shooting off the ground. These types of motion are very fast.

Some of the motion of the space shuttle is very slow. This type of motion happens on the ground.

Scientists work on the shuttle in a building that is about 4 miles from the launch pad. Before it can go to space, the shuttle has to be carried to the launch pad. A kind of truck called the crawler transporter does this job.

A car can travel the distance to the launch pad in just a few minutes. Some people can run it in less than 30 minutes.

The crawler takes quite a bit longer. When it is empty, it can make the trip in 2 hours. It travels at a speed of about 2 miles every hour.

Once the heavy shuttle is added, the crawler slows down even more. It moves to the launch pad in about 5 hours!

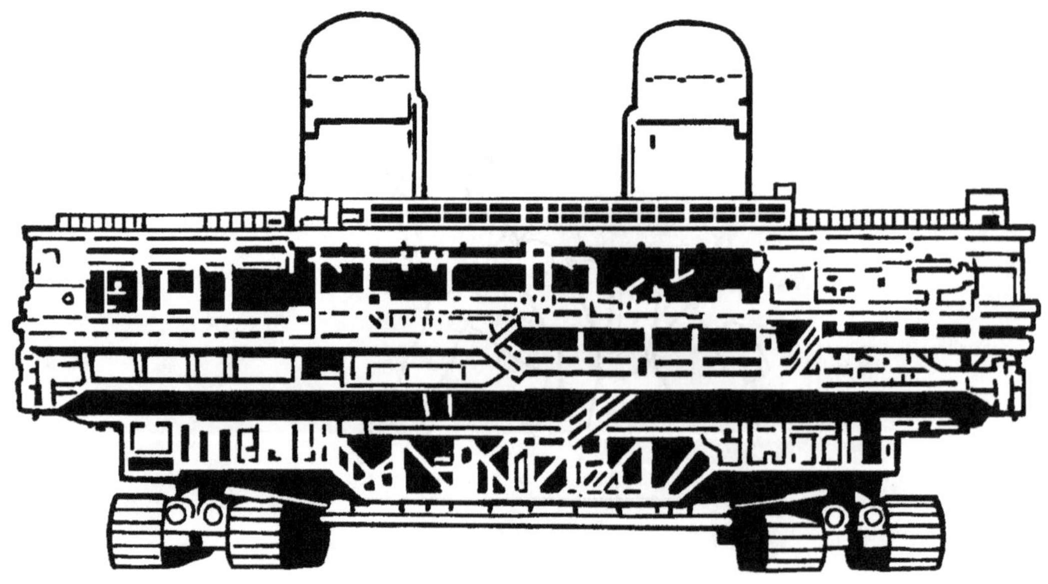

1. Which of these will take the longest to move to the launch pad?

   (A) crawler

   (B) person running

   (C) car

2. What is the job of the crawler?

   (A) to launch the shuttle into space

   (B) to bring the shuttle to the launch pad

   (C) to lift people into the shuttle

3. There are 4 miles between the building and the launch pad. This is a measure of

   (A) time.

   (B) volume.

   (C) distance.

4. How does the speed of the crawler change when the shuttle is added to it?

   (A) It does not change.

   (B) It speeds up.

   (C) It slows down.

5. Where does the space shuttle move the slowest?

   (A) in space

   (B) on the ground

   (C) shooting off the ground into space

Lesson 2
Experiment: Investigating Motion

Speed depends on distance and time. In this activity, you will find out how.

What You Will Need

masking tape

marker

Procedure

1. Place a piece of tape on the floor on one side of the room. Write "Start" on the tape.

2. Place a second piece of tape on the floor on the other side of the room. Write "End" on the tape.

3. Stand behind the tape with a partner.

4. Say "Go." One of you should take a giant step. The other should take a tiny step.

5. Both partners should take steps until they reach the tape marked "End." Each person should take the same size step every time.

6. Count the number of steps each person takes. Write it in the chart.

Experiment: Investigating Motion (cont'd.)

Analysis

PERSON	Number of steps
1 (tiny steps)	
2 (giant steps)	

Who reached the end first?

Conclusion

1. Which person walked faster?

2. How do you know?

3. How would the results change if both people took the same size steps?

Lesson 3 Light, Heat, Electricity, and Magnetism

Have you ever felt as if you had a lot of energy? Or maybe you felt like you were all out of energy. In science, **energy** is the ability to make things change.

You get your energy from the foods you eat, but energy comes in all different forms. One form of energy is light.

You use light to see the things around you. Much of the light you use comes from the sun. The sun is known as a source of light. Other sources of light are stars, light bulbs, and fire.

energy—the ability to cause change

ray—a straight path of light

heat—the flow of thermal energy from a warmer object to a cooler one

charge—an electrical force that can be either positive (+) or negative (−)

electric current—the flow of electric charge

circuit—a path through which electric current can flow

magnet—an object that can push or pull some types of matter

pole—a region of a magnet where the magnetic effects are strongest

© Harcourt Achieve Inc. All rights reserved.

How Light Behaves

Have you ever shined a flashlight in the dark? The light goes where you point the flashlight. Light travels in straight lines called **rays**.

What happens when light hits an object? The answer depends on the type of object. Light bounces off of some objects. A mirror is this type of object.

Some objects let light pass through them. A window is this type of object. If light hits a window at a slant, it changes speed. The change in speed causes the light to bend. Objects can look bent when light bends. Look at the pencil in the glass of water below.

What Is Heat?

You feel chilly on a cold day. What do you do? Maybe you put on a sweater. A sweater slows down the loss of heat from your body. **Heat** is the flow of energy.

This type of energy is different from light energy. It is called thermal energy. All objects have thermal energy. Some objects have more thermal energy than others. An object has more thermal energy when it is warm than when it is cold.

Heat flows from a warmer object to a cooler one. When you are warm, heat flows from you to the air. When you give up heat, you become colder.

The opposite happens for ice cream. Try to eat an ice-cream cone on a hot day. The air is warmer than the ice cream. Heat flows from the warm air to the cold ice cream. This causes the ice cream to become warmer and melt.

Electricity

A storm forms on a summer afternoon. Bright lightning crackles in the sky. Lightning happens when clouds give up an electric charge. An electric **charge** is a property of matter.

All matter is made up of smaller particles that you cannot see. Some particles have a plus (+) charge. Others have a minus (−) charge. Some particles do not have any electric charge.

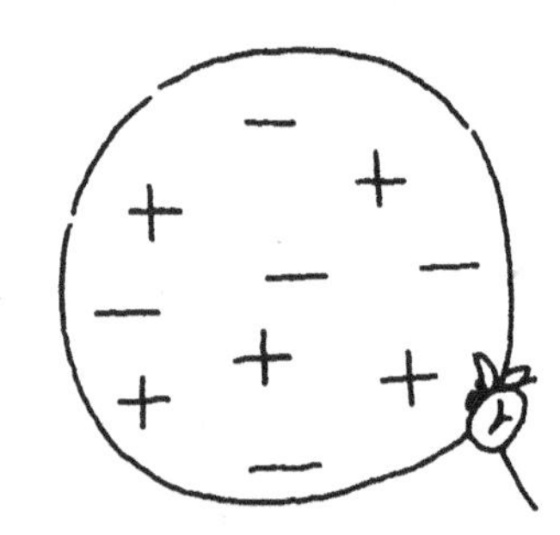

Sometimes, extra charges build up on an object. This is called static electricity. When an object with static electricity gives up its extra charge, a spark can occur. Lightning is a large spark caused when rain clouds give up their extra charge.

www.harcourtschoolsupply.com
© Harcourt Achieve Inc. All rights reserved.

Lesson 3, Light, Heat, Electricity, and Magnetism
Science 2, SV 9781419034305

Electric Current

In some objects, electric charges flow from one place to another. The flow of electric charges is called **electric current**.

Electric charges can only flow through certain materials. Charges can flow through metal wires. A path that an electric current can flow through is called a **circuit**.

All of the electric devices you use are part of a circuit. Radios, televisions, and lights are all parts of circuits.

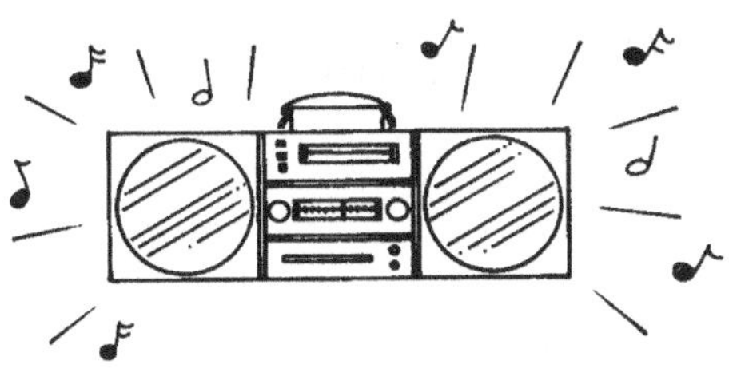

Magnetism

Have you ever played with toys that have magnets on them? Maybe you found that the toys could pull each other together. Maybe they could also push each other apart. A **magnet** is an object that can push or pull some types of matter.

Magnets come in different shapes. Some magnets are long and thin. Other magnets are shaped like a horseshoe. All magnets have two regions called **poles**. One pole is known as the north pole and the other is the south pole. The push or pull of a magnet is strongest at the poles.

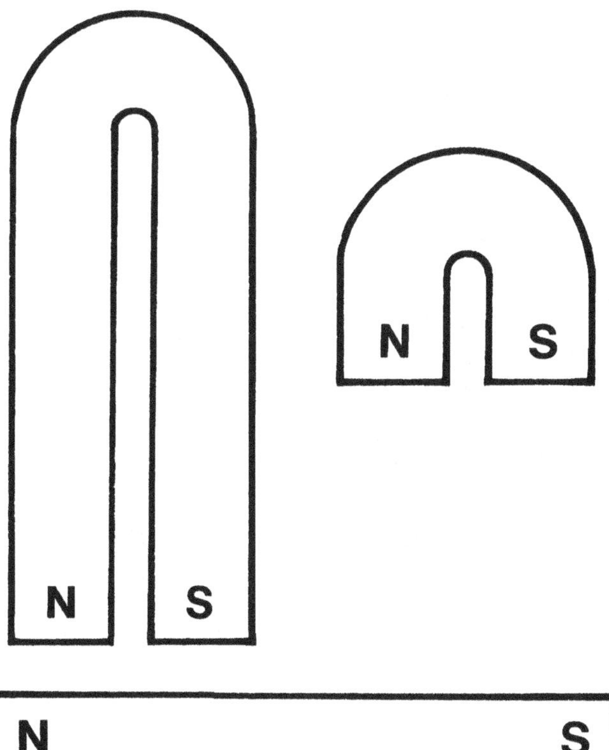

© Harcourt Achieve Inc. All rights reserved.

Lesson 3   Review

Darken the circle by the best answer.

1. What is energy?

Ⓐ the ability to cause change

Ⓑ the pull between two objects

Ⓒ the size of an object

2. What happens when light hits a mirror?

Ⓐ It disappears.

Ⓑ It passes through.

Ⓒ It bounces off.

3. Why does a pencil in a glass of water look bent?

Ⓐ Light changes speed in the glass.

Ⓑ The pencil breaks in water.

Ⓒ The pencil gives off heat.

4. What is an electric current?

Ⓐ charges that build up

Ⓑ moving electric charges

Ⓒ heat moving from an object

5. What happens at the poles of a magnet?

Ⓐ The magnet is strongest.

Ⓑ The magnet is broken.

Ⓒ The magnet is connected to something.

6. A hot spoon is placed in a cold metal sink. In which direction will heat flow between the spoon and the sink? Why?

____

____

____

____

www.harcourtschoolsupply.com
© Harcourt Achieve Inc. All rights reserved.

Lesson 3 — Light

Light can move through some things, such as a window. Some things block the light so it cannot go through, such as a book. Some things let a small amount of light through, such as wax paper.

Tell if light can move through each thing. Write <u>all</u>, <u>some</u>, or <u>none</u> under each picture.

1.

____

2.

____

3.
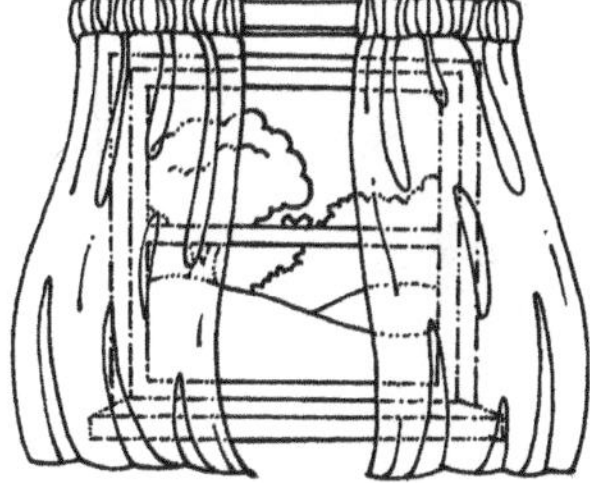

____

4.
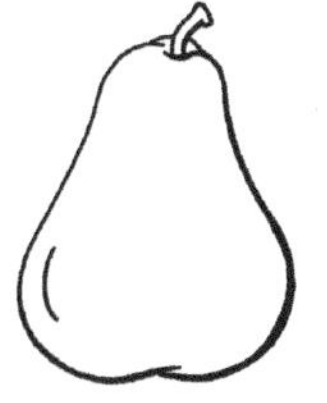

____

5.

____

6.

____

7.

____

8.
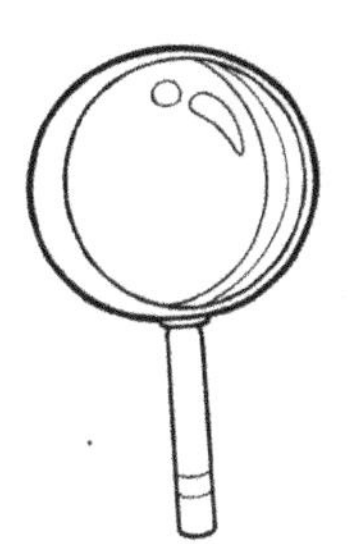

____

9.

____

www.harcourtschoolsupply.com
© Harcourt Achieve Inc. All rights reserved.

Lesson 3, Light
Science 2, SV 9781419034305

Lesson 3   Movement of Light

The arrows show light moving toward two objects. Object A is a mirror. Object B is a window. Draw another arrow to show how light moves after it hits each object.

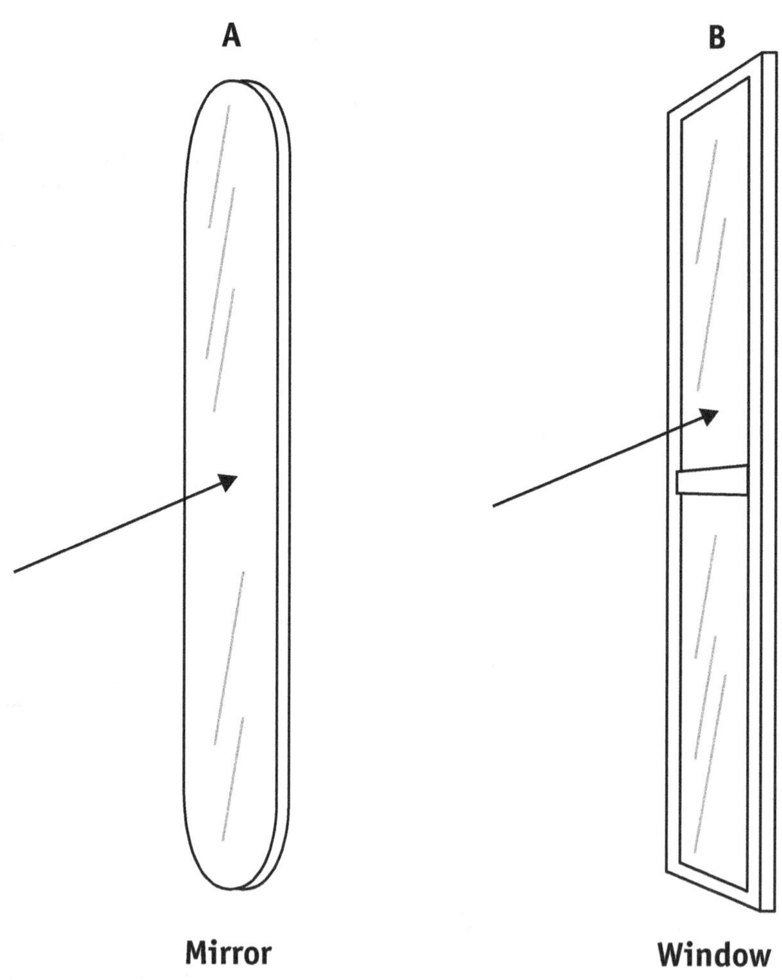

Lesson 3
Heat Flow

Each picture shows two objects. Draw an arrow between each pair of objects to show which way heat will flow between them.

1.  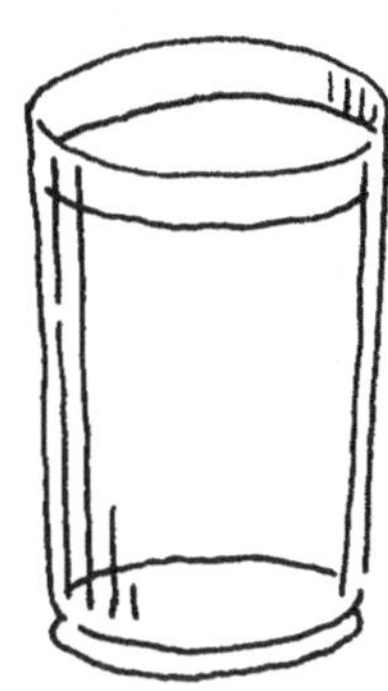

2. 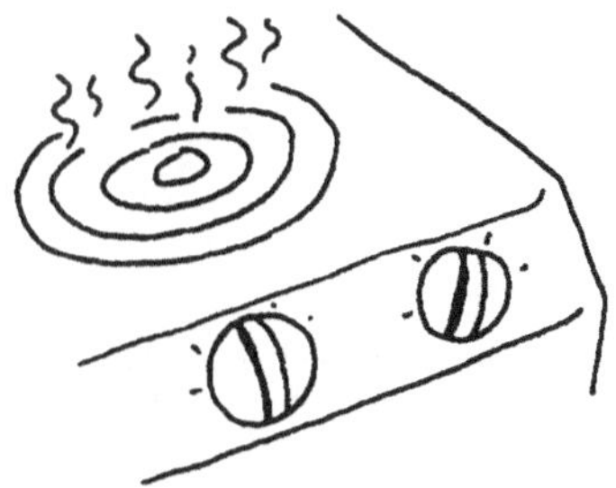 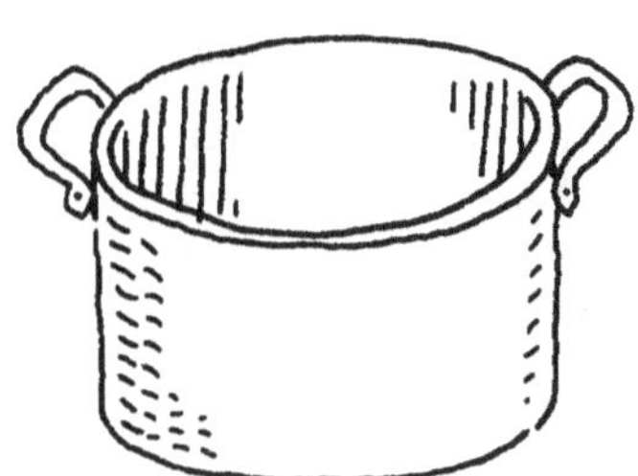

3.  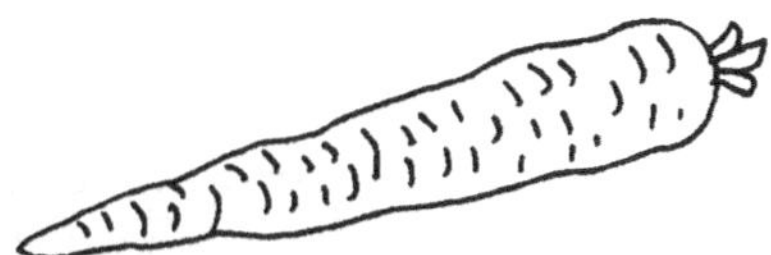

4.  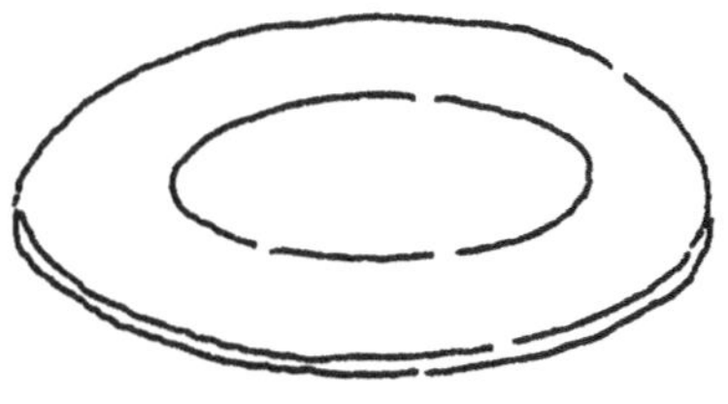

Lesson 3

Heat Change

People often use heat when they cook. Heat is a form of energy that can change matter. If you heat ice, it will change the solid ice to liquid water. If you heat an egg, the egg will become a solid. If you heat bread by toasting it, the bread will turn brown and get harder.

Heat makes some changes that can be reversed, or changed back. Some of the changes cannot be reversed.

Color the pictures that show the matter that has been changed by heat.

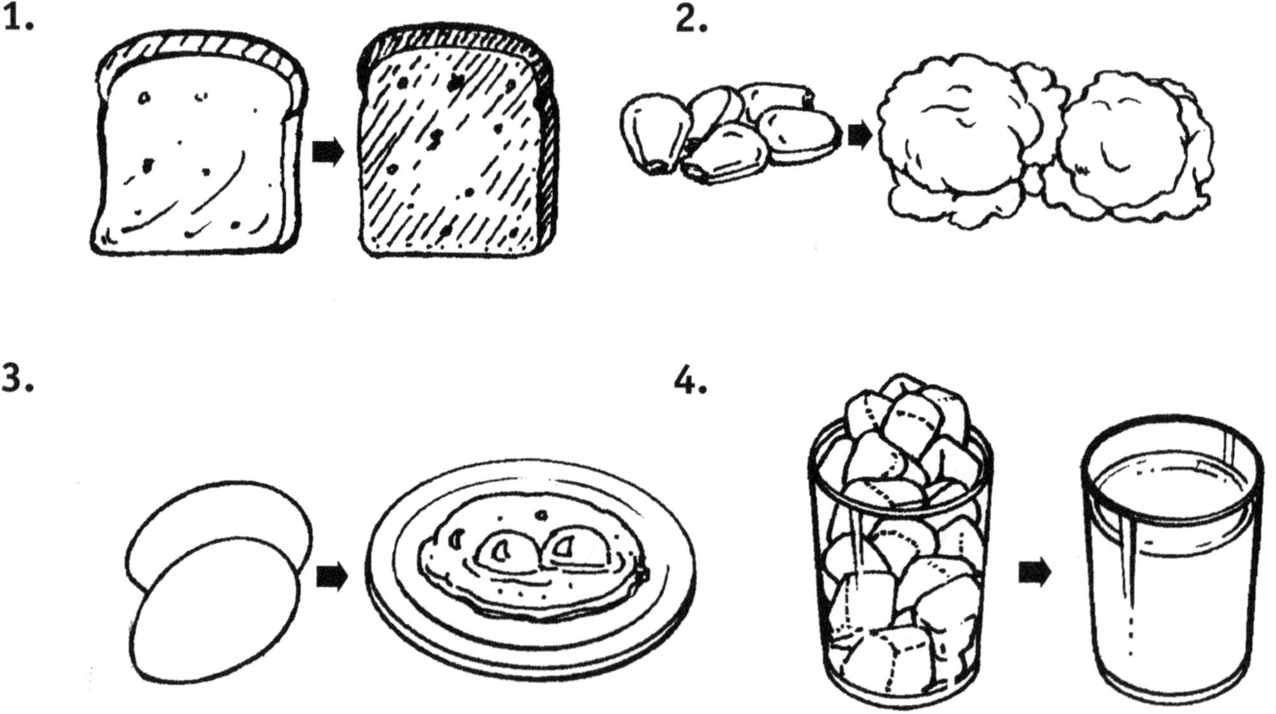

1.

2.

3.

4.

Lesson 3   Types of Energy

Each word in the column on the left is related to a word or group of words on the right. Draw a line connecting the matching words.

ray	circuit
charge	thermal energy
magnet	electrical force
heat	light
current	pole

Use the words in sentences of your own.

____

____

____

____

____

____

____

www.harcourtschoolsupply.com
© Harcourt Achieve Inc. All rights reserved.

Lesson 3   A Compass

Read the following passage. Then answer the questions that follow the passage.

Many people use a compass to find direction. A compass is a tool that has a thin needle in it. The needle is a magnet. It is able to spin in all directions.

A compass spins until it points toward the north. The reason is that Earth acts like a giant magnet. It has a north pole and a south pole.

A compass points toward the north pole. Once you know which way is north, you can figure out the other directions.

Long before sailors had good maps, they used compasses to sail around the world. People who hike also use compasses. Today, there are electric devices that people can use to find their way. Even so, many people still rely on their trusty compass.

1. What makes a compass work?
   (A) a magnet
   (B) electric current
   (C) light

2. In which direction does a compass point?
   (A) south
   (B) west
   (C) north

3. Why might a person use a compass?
   (A) to tell which way to go
   (B) to turn on an electric device
   (C) to keep a room warm

4. Which of these is most likely to be used along with a compass?
   (A) a comb
   (B) a map
   (C) a sandwich

Lesson 3   Experiment: Investigating Light

Light is all around you. In this activity, you will show that light travels in straight lines.

What You Will Need

small flashlight
4 large index cards
clay
hole punch

Procedure

1. Punch or make a hole in the center of three of the index cards.

2. Mold the clay into four small balls.

3. Put each card into a ball of clay so that the cards stand up on a desk or counter.

4. Arrange the cards in a row so that the holes line up. The card without the hole should be at the end of the line.

5. Dim the lights in the room. Turn on the flashlight and shine it on the first card. Look to see if the light reaches the last card.

6. Move one of the cards a few centimeters to one side. Repeat Step 5.

Experiment: Investigating Light (cont'd.)

Analysis

1. Did the light reach the last card when the holes were all in a line?

____

2. Did the light reach the last card when one index card was moved to the side?

____

Conclusion

Does light travel in straight lines?

____

Lesson 4 Characteristics of Organisms

Living things and nonliving things are all around you. A **living** thing is something that is alive. It grows and changes. A **nonliving** thing is not alive. It does not grow and change.

Sometimes it is easy to tell whether something is living. When you see a fish swimming, you know it is living. Other times, it is not as easy to decide. A tree does not move or make noise. A tree is still a living thing. To decide if something is living or nonliving, you must know the characteristics of living things.

Organisms Have Traits in Common

All organisms are made up of smaller parts. The smaller parts are called cells. A **cell** is the basic unit of life.

Some organisms are made of only one cell. Others are made of many cells.

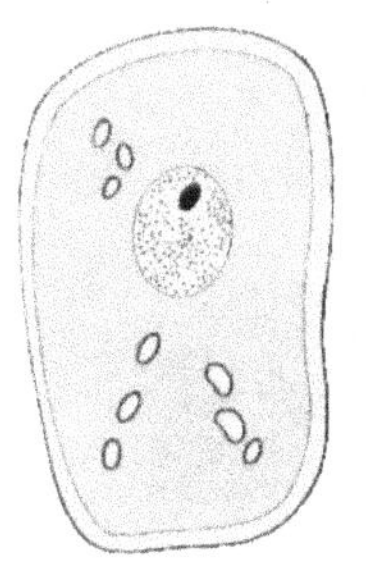

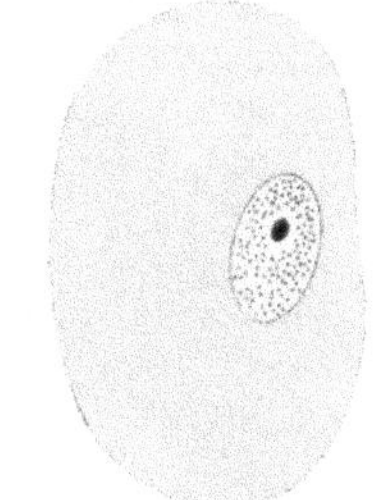

Plant Cell   Animal Cell

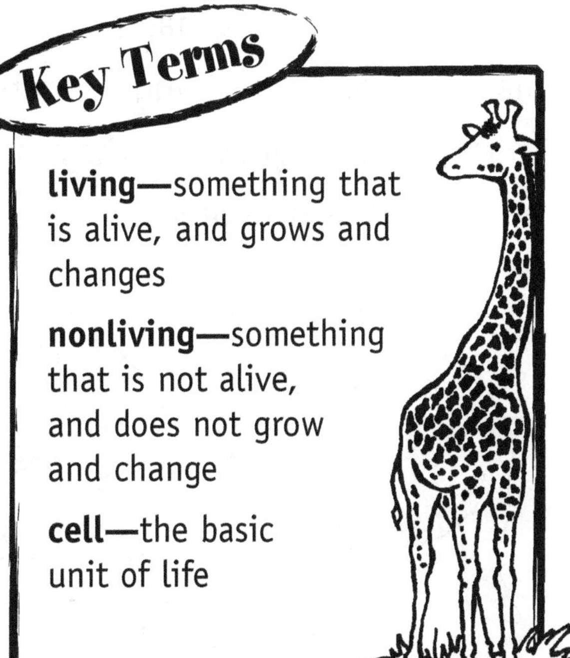

www.harcourtschoolsupply.com
© Harcourt Achieve Inc. All rights reserved.

Lesson 4, Characteristics of Organisms
Science 2, SV 9781419034305

When you hear a noise, you might turn your head. You <u>react</u> to the noise. All organisms can react to things around them.

Some frogs bury themselves in mud when they get too warm. Many birds fly south when it gets too cold. Some trees lose their leaves in the fall.

Living things can make more living things. When a dog has puppies, it makes more living things. When those puppies grow up, they might have their own puppies.

Over time, puppies grow up. You too will grow up. You started as a small baby. Now you are a young person. At some point, all organisms grow and change.

Organisms Share the Same Needs

Living things need nonliving things. One nonliving thing they need is energy. Some living things get energy from sunlight. Plants get energy this way. Other living things get energy from the foods they eat. Animals get energy this way.

Living things also need water. Water carries materials through a living thing. Much of your body is made up of water. This is why it is important for you to drink water each day.

Do you ever sweat when you are hot? Sweating is a way that humans cool off. Humans and many other living things must not get too hot. They also need to keep from getting too cold. When you shiver on a cold day, it helps your body keep warm.

Many other living things get as warm or cold as their surroundings. Lizards are an example of this type of living thing.

When lizards become cool, they lie in the sun to get warm. When they are too warm, they move to shady places to get cool.

You cannot stay underwater for too long. You need to breathe air. When you breathe in, your body takes oxygen from air. Oxygen is a gas that your cells need. Many living things need air in the same way.

When you breathe out, you release carbon dioxide. This is a gas that plants need. Plants give off oxygen.

Organisms also need space. All organisms need a place to live and grow. Some organisms live in small spaces. Others need much more space to move around.

www.harcourtschoolsupply.com
© Harcourt Achieve Inc. All rights reserved.

Lesson 4, Characteristics of Organisms
Science 2, SV 9781419034305

Lesson 4   **Review**

Darken the circle by the best answer.

1. How is a nonliving thing different from a living thing?

   Ⓐ It is not found in air.

   Ⓑ It is not found in water.

   Ⓒ It does not grow and change.

2. What is a cell?

   Ⓐ the basic unit of life

   Ⓑ the place where an organism lives

   Ⓒ a food that an organism eats

3. Which of these does NOT describe a characteristic of all organisms?

   Ⓐ They are made of cells.

   Ⓑ They grow and change.

   Ⓒ They can move.

4. How do animals get energy?

   Ⓐ by sitting in the sun

   Ⓑ by eating foods

   Ⓒ by sleeping

5. Which of these actions will help a person cool off?

   Ⓐ sweating

   Ⓑ rubbing hands together

   Ⓒ jumping up and down

6. What do plants release into the air that animals need?

   Ⓐ carbon dioxide

   Ⓑ oxygen

   Ⓒ soil

7. How can you tell that a bean plant is living?

____

____

____

www.harcourtschoolsupply.com
© Harcourt Achieve Inc. All rights reserved.

Lesson 4
Living and Nonliving Things

Look at the things in the pictures below. Write an <u>L</u> under a picture if it shows something that is living. Write an <u>N</u> under a picture if it shows something that is nonliving.

1. 

2. 

3. 

4. 

5. 

6. 

7. 

8. 

9. 

10. 

www.harcourtschoolsupply.com
© Harcourt Achieve Inc. All rights reserved.

Lesson 4, Living and Nonliving Things
Science 2, SV 9781419034305

Lesson 4 — Living Things

Each picture shows a characteristic of living things. Write the word or group of words that best describes each picture. Choose from the list below.

cells	grows and changes	makes more living things
needs energy	needs water	reacts

1. 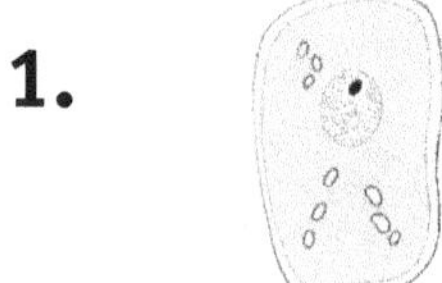 _______________________________________

2.  _______________________________________

3.  _______________________________________

4.  _______________________________________

5.  _______________________________________

6.  _______________________________________

www.harcourtschoolsupply.com
© Harcourt Achieve Inc. All rights reserved.

Lesson 4   Living Things Around Me

Go on a hunt around your home. Look for living and nonliving things.

In the chart below, draw a picture of each living thing on the left side. Draw a picture of each nonliving thing on the right side.

Compare the things you put on each side of the chart.

Things Around Me

Living	Nonliving

Lesson 4 — Coral Reefs

Read the following passage. Then answer the questions that follow the passage.

Some of the most beautiful living things in the world live in coral reefs. If you felt a coral reef, you might think a coral reef is nonliving like a rock. You might be surprised to find out that a coral reef is made from parts of living things.

Tiny animals called coral polyps make shells. When the animals die, the shells are left behind. New polyps make new shells on top of old shells. This is how a coral reef grows bigger.

Corals live in warm water. Coral reefs are found in shallow water. The water cannot be very deep because corals reefs need sunlight, too.

Corals come in many different colors and shapes. Some look like horns. Others look like brains. Some even look like flowers.

Many different kinds of fish live in a coral reef. Like the coral, the fish have different colors and shapes. The clown fish is orange with white stripes. The sea horse looks like a horse that can swim. The lion fish looks like it has a lion's mane. What do you think the starfish looks like? That's right, it looks like a star.

www.harcourtschoolsupply.com
© Harcourt Achieve Inc. All rights reserved.

1. What is a coral reef?

  (A) a tree

  (B) a pile of sand

  (C) shells from living things

2. How does a coral reef grow?

  (A) A coral polyp gets bigger.

  (B) New coral polyps make new shells.

  (C) Fish live on the reef.

3. Where would you expect to find a coral reef?

  (A) in warm, shallow water

  (B) in mountain streams

  (C) in freshwater lakes

4. Which sentence about corals is true?

  (A) All corals have the same shape.

  (B) All corals are the same color.

  (C) Corals come in many shapes and colors.

5. Coral polyps are

  (A) animals.

  (B) plants.

  (C) rocks.

www.harcourtschoolsupply.com
© Harcourt Achieve Inc. All rights reserved.

Lesson 4   Experiment: Looking at Living Things

Living things have many of the same characteristics. In this activity, you will look for some of those characteristics.

What You Will Need

a living thing you can watch (examples include a fish in a tank, a bird in a nearby tree, a pet in your home or classroom, or even a family member)

Procedure

1. Write down the date and time. Watch the living thing for several minutes.

2. Write down what the living thing does.

3. Repeat steps 1 and 2 at different times of the day for five days.

Analysis

Date and Time	Notes

© Harcourt Achieve Inc. All rights reserved.

Experiment: Looking at Living Things (cont'd.)

1. Did the living thing eat?

____

2. Did the living thing react to something?

____

3. Did the living thing take in air?

____

Conclusion

What are some of the characteristics of the living thing you watched?

____

____

____

www.harcourtschoolsupply.com
© Harcourt Achieve Inc. All rights reserved.

Lesson 5 Life Cycles of Organisms

A kangaroo begins as a tiny baby called a joey. After it is born, it lives in its mother's pouch. Once it grows, the joey leaves the pouch and moves on its own.

Like other animals, a kangaroo grows and changes until it looks like its parents. The parts of an animal's life from the time it is born until it dies make up its **life cycle**.

Life Cycle of a Bird

The life cycle of a bird begins with an **egg**. A mother bird lays eggs. She sits on them to keep them warm.

Sometimes the father bird sits on them instead.

A chick grows inside its egg. When it gets big enough, it breaks the eggshell and hatches. The young bird looks different from its parents. The

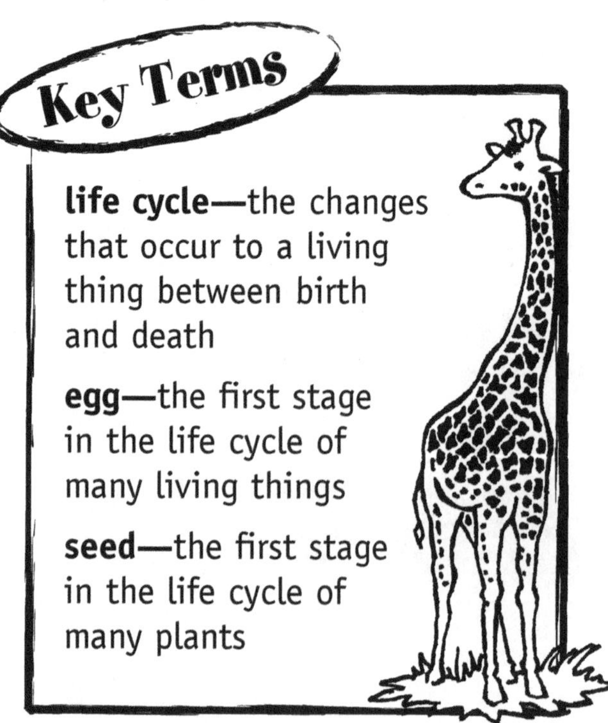

Key Terms

life cycle—the changes that occur to a living thing between birth and death

egg—the first stage in the life cycle of many living things

seed—the first stage in the life cycle of many plants

www.harcourtschoolsupply.com
© Harcourt Achieve Inc. All rights reserved.

parent birds give their babies food when they are young.

The young bird gets larger and larger. As it grows, it gets new feathers. In time, it looks like its parents.

Life Cycle of Mammals

Elephants are examples of mammals. Most mammals are not born in eggs. They start growing inside their mothers' bodies. When they are big enough, they are born.

Mammals do not eat solid food when they are first born. Young mammals drink milk from their mother. The milk gives them what they need to grow. When they are grown, mammals look and eat like their parents.

Life Cycles of Other Organisms

Some living things change as they grow. Their young forms look very different from their adult forms. Some living things even live in different places as they grow. One such organism is a frog.

Frogs lay eggs in water. The eggs hatch into tadpoles. A tadpole is like a fish because it can live in water. The tadpole grows quickly. In time, the tadpole grows legs. Its tail goes away. Over time, the tadpole becomes a frog that can live on land.

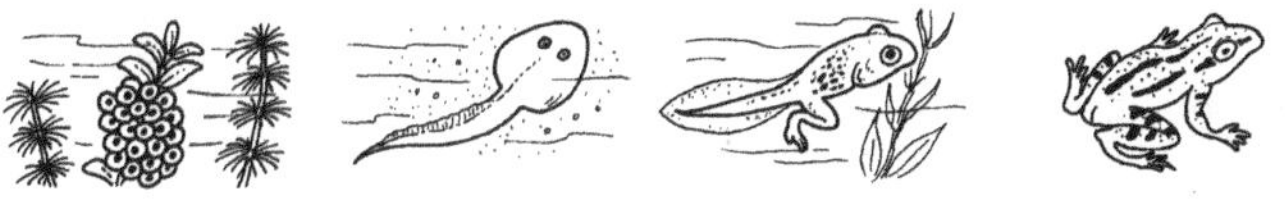

Many insects go through big changes, too. A butterfly begins as an egg. Then it turns into a caterpillar.

After a while, it makes a cocoon around itself. While it is inside, the caterpillar grows and changes. When it comes out, it is a butterfly.

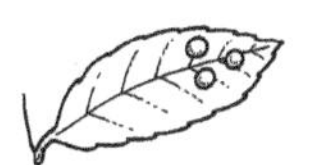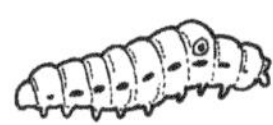

www.harcourtschoolsupply.com
© Harcourt Achieve Inc. All rights reserved.

Life Cycles of Plants

What is the first thing you do to plant a vegetable garden? You might get seeds. A **seed** is the first stage in the life cycle of a plant that makes flowers.

If the seed gets everything it needs, it will sprout. A seedling will grow. With the right amount of light, water, air, and soil, the seedling will grow into an adult plant.

Some plants begin as seeds that do not come from flowers. Have you ever seen a pine cone? A pine cone comes from a pine tree. This type of plant makes seeds in cones. When the seeds are ready, the cone opens up. This lets the seeds blow away.

www.harcourtschoolsupply.com
© Harcourt Achieve Inc. All rights reserved.

Lesson 5, Life Cycles of Organisms
Science 2, SV 9781419034305

Lesson 5   **Review**

Darken the circle by the best answer.

1. What does the life cycle of an organism describe?

   Ⓐ how much space it takes up

   Ⓑ what it needs to eat to survive

   Ⓒ how it changes from birth to death

2. What is the first stage in the life cycle of a bird?

   Ⓐ a nest

   Ⓑ an egg

   Ⓒ a worm

3. How do most mammals begin their lives?

   Ⓐ growing inside their mothers' bodies

   Ⓑ developing inside eggs

   Ⓒ swimming as tadpoles

4. What happens inside a cocoon?

   Ⓐ A tadpole turns into a frog.

   Ⓑ A seed grows into a plant.

   Ⓒ A caterpillar turns into a butterfly.

5. Where are the seeds of a pine tree made?

   Ⓐ in flowers

   Ⓑ in cones

   Ⓒ in leaves

6. What do all mammals have in common about the food they eat when they are young?

   ____

   ____

   ____

Lesson 5   Growing Up

The pictures show a lion growing. Pretend that you work at a zoo and get to see the lion grow up. Write a short letter to a friend telling about the changes you see.

Dear ____________________,

____

____

____

____

Your friend,

____

Lesson 5   Butterfly Life Cycle

The pictures show the life cycle of a butterfly. Write the name of each stage on the lines. Choose from the list below.

butterfly	egg	cocoon	caterpillar

1.

____

2.

____

3.

____

4.

____

© Harcourt Achieve Inc. All rights reserved.

Lesson 5   Seeds

Seeds come in all different sizes and shapes. Gather several different kinds of seeds. Look at the seeds carefully. Use a hand lens if you have one.

Draw a picture of each type of seed. Write a few words describing the seed. Tell about its shape and color. Tell what type of plant the seed will grow into.

Seed 1	Seed 2	Seed 3

Seed 4	Seed 5	Seed 6

Lesson 5

Seeds We Eat

People eat many foods that are seeds.

Circle the foods that are seeds.

www.harcourtschoolsupply.com
© Harcourt Achieve Inc. All rights reserved.

Lesson 5, Seeds We Eat
Science 2, SV 9781419034305

Lesson 5

Experiment: Investigating the Life Cycle of a Plant

Living things grow and change. Some start as eggs. Others start as seeds. In this activity, you will find out about the life cycle of a plant.

What You Will Need

seeds from a flowering plant

foam cup or flowerpot

water

potting soil

Procedure

1. Fill a cup or flowerpot partway with potting soil.

2. Push several seeds into the soil.

3. Water the seeds. Do not give them too much water.

4. Place the pot in a place where it will get sunlight for part of the day.

5. Water the seeds each day.

6. Each day for two weeks, check the seeds. Write or draw any changes you see.

Experiment: Investigating the Life Cycle of a Plant (cont'd.)

Analysis

Day	How Plant Looks
1	
2	
3	

Where did the seeds you used come from?

____

____

Conclusion

What are the stages in the life cycle of a plant?

____

____

Lesson 6 Living Things and Environments

How would you describe the environment where you live? An **environment** is made up of all the living and nonliving things in a place. Some of the living things around you might include plants, animals, and people. Your home, toys, and clothes are some of the nonliving things in your environment.

Habitats

Many different living things might be in the same environment. The specific place where an organism finds the things it needs to live is called a **habitat**.

environment—the living and nonliving things in a place

habitat—a place where an organism finds the things it needs to live

desert—an environment that does not get much rain

rain forest—a warm environment that gets rain all year long

forest—an environment that gets enough rain for many trees to grow

tundra—a cold, dry environment

pond—a freshwater environment

ocean—a large body of salt water

food chain—a diagram that shows how energy moves from plants to animals

www.harcourtschoolsupply.com
© Harcourt Achieve Inc. All rights reserved.

An environment may have several different habitats. Some habitats are on land, and others are in water.

In a forest, a group of trees might be the habitat of a bird. The soil might be the habitat of a worm. A large area of the forest might be the habitat of a deer. Different animals might share the same habitat.

Desert

A **desert** is an environment that does not get much rain. It is very dry. Only a few types of plants and animals can live in a desert.

A cactus is one type of desert plant. It can live without a lot of water. Many desert plants can save water to use when they need it. Some animals that live in the desert can get water from the foods they eat.

Rain Forest

A **rain forest** is an environment that gets a lot of rain. In a rain forest, it rains almost every day. The weather in a rain forest is warm all year long. There are many plants in a rain forest. They make the forest thick and green.

Many animals live in a rain forest. More kinds of plants and animals live in a rain forest than in any other environment.

Forests

Other types of **forests** get more rain than deserts, but less than rain forests. These other forests are often cold for part of the year. They are warm for the other part. Many trees can grow in these forests. Animals use the trees for food and shelter.

The trees of some forests lose their leaves in the fall. Before they do, the leaves turn beautiful colors of orange, red, and yellow. When winter ends, new leaves grow on the trees.

Some animals leave the forest during the winter. They move to warmer places. They come back after the winter ends.

Tundra

The **tundra** is a very cold environment. It is also windy and does not get much rain. Ice and snow cover the ground for most of the year. Only a few small plants can grow in the tundra.

Animals that live in the tundra need to be able to stay warm. Polar bears have thick fur that helps them survive there. Seals and whales have a layer of fat called blubber that keeps them warm.

Freshwater Environments

A **pond** is a freshwater environment. Many animals live in a pond. There

www.harcourtschoolsupply.com
© Harcourt Achieve Inc. All rights reserved.

are turtles and fish in the water. There are frogs, birds, and otters along the edges of the pond.

Some plants live on top of the pond. Many animals use these plants as shelter. Others use these plants for food. Some plants live in the water of a pond. Fish use these plants for shelter and food.

Saltwater Environments

An **ocean** is a large body of salt water. Different kinds of plants and animals live in salt water than live in fresh water. Living things called algae live near the top of the ocean. They are food for fish and other ocean animals.

Some ocean animals come near the top to find food. Other animals come to the top to get air. Dolphins and whales do this.

Fish do not need to come to the top. They breathe in the water through their gills. Other animals stay on the ocean floor. Lobsters and crabs do this.

Food Chain

Living things in all environments need energy. Remember that plants get the energy they need from sunlight. They use this energy to make food.

Some animals eat plants for food. Other animals eat animals that have eaten plants.

Each time an animal eats, it gets energy from its food. The **food chain** on the next page shows how energy passes from plants to animals.

Food Chain

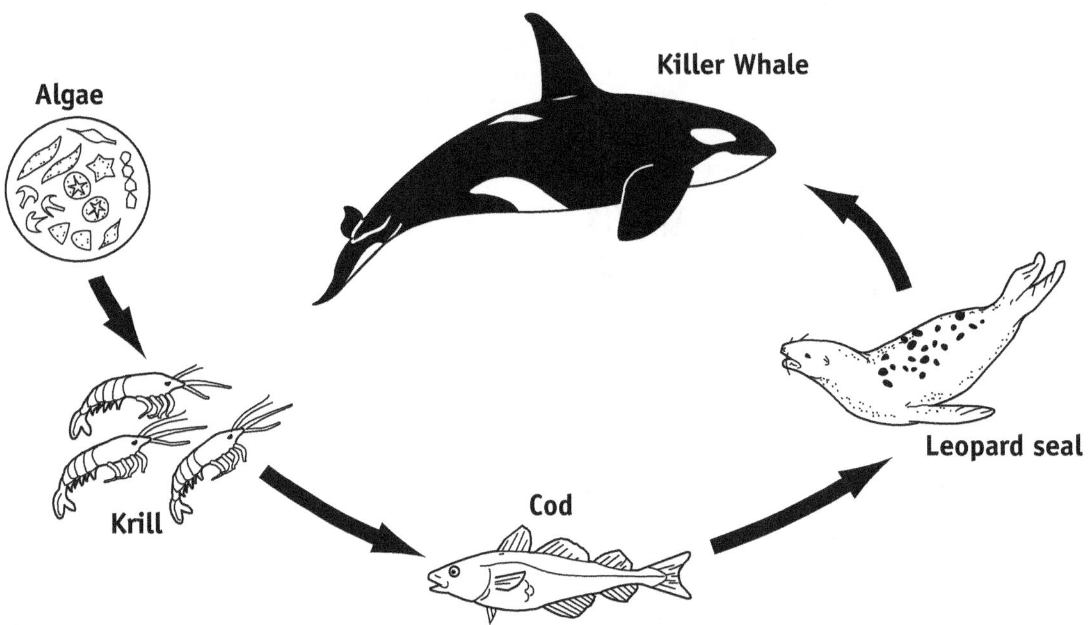

www.harcourtschoolsupply.com
© Harcourt Achieve Inc. All rights reserved.

Lesson 6, Living Things and Environments
Science 2, SV 9781419034305

Lesson 6   Review

Darken the circle by the best answer.

1. All of the living and nonliving things in a place make up

   (A) an environment.

   (B) an organism.

   (C) a food chain.

2. Which of these statements is true?

   (A) A habitat is a kind of organism.

   (B) All living things need a large habitat.

   (C) An environment can have several habitats.

3. A cactus needs only a small amount of water. In which environment would a cactus live?

   (A) rain forest

   (B) desert

   (C) pond

4. Which environment is known for thick, green plants and many animals?

   (A) tundra

   (B) desert

   (C) rain forest

5. A polar bear lives in a cold environment known as the

   (A) tundra.

   (B) desert.

   (C) rain forest.

6. How is an ocean different from a pond?

   (A) An ocean has fish in it.

   (B) An ocean is made of salt water.

   (C) An ocean has plants in it.

7. What helps polar bears survive in the tundra?

   ____

   ____

Lesson 6

Wet or Dry?

Read about the desert and the rain forest.

This is a **desert**. The hot sun heats up the dry sand and rocks. There is little or no water around because it doesn't rain much in a desert. Few plants can grow there.

Desert

This is a **rain forest**. It rains almost every day in a rain forest. Water drips from the leaves of plants. It flows in rivers and streams. Many plants grow in this habitat.

Rain forest

Circle the word that tells about each habitat.

1. desert   dry   wet

2. rain forest   dry   wet

www.harcourtschoolsupply.com
© Harcourt Achieve Inc. All rights reserved.

Lesson 6

Where Things Live

Fill in the puzzle with the terms described by each clue. Choose from the word box below.

blubber	cactus	desert	environment	food
forest	ocean	pond	sunlight	tundra

Across

2. an environment that has many trees in it
4. a large body of salt water
8. the living and nonliving things in a place
10. a cold, dry environment

Down

1. a layer of fat that keeps animals warm in very cold environments
3. the source of energy for green plants
5. a plant that grows in the desert
6. a very dry environment that often has sand
7. A _________________ chain is a diagram showing the flow of energy from plants to animals.
9. a freshwater environment with plants and animals

Lesson 6   **Different Habitats**

The pictures below show different types of animals. Match the animals to the environments listed. Draw a line matching each animal to its environment.

1.    ocean

2.    tundra

3.    forest

4.    desert

5.    pond

6.    rain forest

www.harcourtschoolsupply.com
© Harcourt Achieve Inc. All rights reserved.

Lesson 6 Ant Habitat

Read about where some ants live.

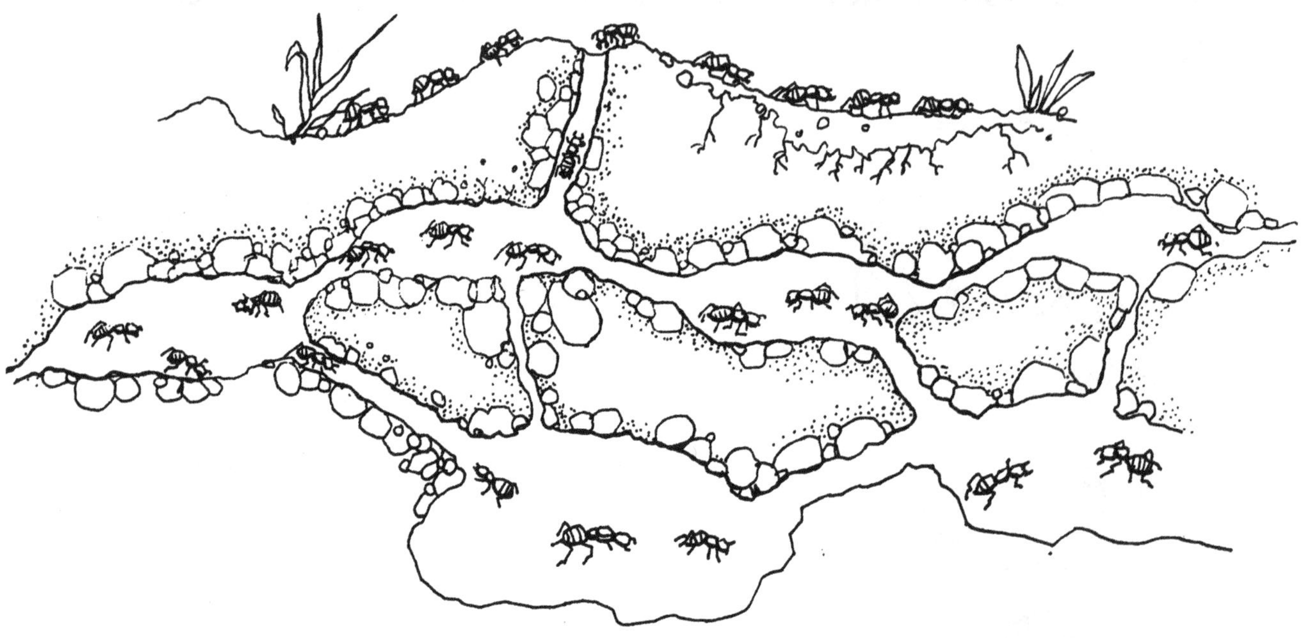

Some insects, like ants, live and work in large groups. The group is called a colony. The ants might build nests underground. The nests have many rooms and tunnels. The soil underground is the ants' habitat.

Answer the questions.

1. How many rooms are in this colony?

____

2. How many ants can you see in this colony?

____

Lesson 6   Ocean Food Chain

Number the pictures to show the order of a food chain. Then answer the questions.

1. What would happen to the small fish if the plants were gone?

____

____

2. What would happen to the big fish if the small fish were gone?

____

____

3. If the plants were gone, would the people catch any fish?

____

____

4. Why do all living things need plants?

____

____

www.harcourtschoolsupply.com
© Harcourt Achieve Inc. All rights reserved.

Lesson 6, Ocean Food Chain
Science 2, SV 9781419034305

Lesson 6   **The Arctic Hare**

Read the following passage. Then answer the questions that follow the passage.

Living things have traits that help them live in their environment. The arctic hare is a small animal like a rabbit. It has traits that help it live in the tundra.

Large birds eat arctic hares. Wolves, foxes, and polar bears eat them, too. To keep safe, the hare must be hard to see. One trait that makes the arctic hare hard to see is its color.

In the winter, the arctic hare is white. This helps it blend into the white snow.

The tundra has a short summer. In some parts of the tundra, the snow melts during summer. The ground is gray and brown. During this time, the fur of the arctic hare turns gray and brown. The hare blends into the color of the ground. When snow covers the ground in the winter, the hare turns white again.

1. In which environment does the arctic hare live? _______________________

2. What color is the arctic hare in winter? _______________________

3. What color is the arctic hare in summer? _______________________

4. How do the colors of the arctic hare help it live in its environment?

____

____

Lesson 6   Experiment: Investigating Environments

Living things need to be safe in their environment. One way to be safe is to hide from bigger living things. In this activity, you will find out how the color of a living thing can help keep it safe.

What You Will Need

2 sheets of black paper
2 sheets of white paper
hole punch
pencils

Procedure

1. Use the hole punch to cut 15 circles from each color paper.

2. Drop all of the circles onto the black paper.

3. Say "Go," and ask a partner to pick up 5 circles while you count to 5. Say "Stop" when you are finished counting.

4. Set the circles aside and repeat Step 3 two more times.

5. Count the number of black circles your partner collected. Write the number in the chart.

6. Count the number of white circles your partner collected. Write the number in the chart.

Experiment: Investigating Environments (cont'd.)

Analysis

Number of black circles	Number of white circles

Which color circles were picked up more often?

____

Conclusion

1. How did the black paper affect the color of circles that were picked up?

____

____

2. How do you think the results would change if you put the circles on white paper?

____

____

3. How do you think color helps living things hide in their environments?

____

____

Lesson 7 Properties of Earth Materials

You step on them all the time. You might even skip them into a pond. They are rocks. A **rock** is a nonliving thing that comes from Earth.

A rock is one type of resource. A **resource** is anything people can use. A **natural resource** is found in nature.

People can change rocks to make them more useful. One way to use rocks is to make them into sculptures. Another way is to use them to build roads.

Soil

Soil is another natural resource. You may have used soil if you have ever planted a garden. Plants need soil to grow. Some animals, such as earthworms, make their homes in soil.

People use soil to make bricks called adobe. They mix wet clay and straw. Then they shape them into bricks. The hard bricks can be used to build things, such as houses.

rock—a hard, nonliving thing that comes from Earth

resource—anything people can use

natural resource—something that people can use that is found in nature

transportation—a way that people move things from one place to another

Soil forms when rock wears into small pieces. Water and wind can break rocks into pieces. Soil also contains water and air. It can have bits from living things, too.

Water

Water is another natural resource. People need water to drink. Animals also need water to drink. Plants need water to grow.

People also use water in other ways. They use water for bathing and cleaning clothes, dishes, and cars. Water is also used for cooking.

Water is used for **transportation**, or ways people move things. Boats and ships float on water. People and objects can travel on boats that move on water.

Water can also be used to make electricity. People build huge walls across rivers. These walls are called dams. Dams hold back the river water. When the water is allowed to flow through the dam, it turns a machine. The machine is like a giant fan. When the water hits the blades of the machine, it turns. As it turns, it makes electricity. This electricity is brought to homes and businesses by wires.

www.harcourtschoolsupply.com
© Harcourt Achieve Inc. All rights reserved.

Lesson 7, Properties of Earth Materials
Science 2, SV 9781419034305

Lesson 7   Review

Darken the circle by the best answer.

1. Which of these is NOT a natural resource?

   Ⓐ rock

   Ⓑ soil

   Ⓒ television

2. What do people do with adobe?

   Ⓐ make buildings

   Ⓑ grow plants

   Ⓒ make electricity

3. Which of these animals is most likely to make its home in soil?

   Ⓐ moose

   Ⓑ earthworm

   Ⓒ dog

4. Which types of machines use water?

   Ⓐ boats

   Ⓑ cars

   Ⓒ buses

5. How can water be used to make electricity?

   Ⓐ It can be put into a machine that changes water into electricity.

   Ⓑ It can flow through a dam to turn the blades of a machine that produces electricity.

   Ⓒ It can flow through electric circuits.

6. What are three ways that people use rock?

____

____

____

____

____

Lesson 7   Earth's Materials

Several terms from this lesson are scrambled below. Use the definitions to unscramble each word. Write the term on the line. Then use the term in a sentence of your own.

1. <u>kroc</u>   a hard, nonliving resource

____

2. <u>tttnnspiaaoorr</u> a way that people move things

____

3. <u>osrrceeu</u>   anything people can use

____

4. <u>ilos</u>   a resource that plants grow in

____

5. <u>retaw</u>   a resource people use for cleaning and cooking

____

Lesson 7   Resources on Earth

The passage below has several missing terms. On each line, write the term that will complete the sentence. Choose from the word box below.

adobe	electricity	natural	roads
rock	soil	transportation	water

A (1) _______________________ resource is something found in nature that people can use. One resource can be used to make a sculpture. A sculpture might be made from a large, heavy (2) _______________________. This same resource can be used to build (3) _______________________.

Plants need (4) _______________________ to grow in. This natural resource has other uses, too. Some people use (5) _______________________ bricks to build their houses. These bricks are made from clay and straw.

There are many uses for another resource. People use (6) _______________________ to clean clothes, dishes, and cars. Boats are a form of (7) _______________________ that uses this resource to carry people and things. When this resource flows through a dam, it can make (8) _______________________.

www.harcourtschoolsupply.com
© Harcourt Achieve Inc. All rights reserved.

Lesson 7, Resources on Earth
Science 2, SV 9781419034305

Lesson 7   Mt. Rushmore

Read the following passage. Then answer the questions that follow the passage.

Mt. Rushmore is a sculpture made on the side of a mountain in South Dakota. The sculpture shows the faces of four presidents. They are George Washington, Thomas Jefferson, Theodore Roosevelt, and Abraham Lincoln.

You might wonder why someone would turn a mountain into a sculpture. The reason was to make something amazing that people would want to visit.

It was hard to decide whose faces to put on the sculpture. The people who planned the sculpture decided to use these presidents because they were so important to the United States. Each man was a strong leader. Their faces remind people that all things are possible.

Mt. Rushmore was picked for the sculpture because it is made mostly of granite. This is a smooth rock that does not wear away easily. Only about 1 inch of granite will be worn away every 10,000 years. This means that the sculpture will last for a very long time.

The sculpture was started in 1927. People worked on the sculpture until 1941. Most of the work was done using dynamite. It was used to blow off parts of rock. Then people used smaller tools to make the details of the faces. The sculpture they made is one of most beautiful landmarks in the United States.

1. Where is Mt. Rushmore?

(A) Florida

(B) South Dakota

(C) New York

2. Why did people carve a sculpture on Mt. Rushmore?

(A) They wanted to attract people to see it.

(B) They wanted to make water flow over the mountain.

(C) They wanted to make the mountain smaller.

3. Why was granite a good rock for the sculpture?

(A) It can be carved without using dynamite.

(B) It is easy for visitors to climb.

(C) It does not wear away quickly.

4. About how long did people work on Mt. Rushmore?

(A) 1 year

(B) 14 years

(C) 50 years

www.harcourtschoolsupply.com
© Harcourt Achieve Inc. All rights reserved.

Lesson 7   Experiment: Investigating Soil

It is important to protect Earth's natural resources. One way that soil is lost is by flowing water. In this activity, you will find out how to prevent the loss of soil.

What You Will Need

watering can

soil

3 small plastic containers

small plastic object

marker

Procedure

1. Make a mound of soil in each plastic container. Label the containers 1, 2, and 3.

2. Place a small plastic object along the slope of the mound in container 2.

3. Use your finger to flatten circles around the mound in container 3.

4. Slowly pour water over the mound in container 1. Watch what happens to the soil.

5. Repeat Step 4 for the other two containers.

www.harcourtschoolsupply.com
© Harcourt Achieve Inc. All rights reserved.

Lesson 7, Experiment: Investigating Soil
Science 2, SV 9781419034305

Experiment: Investigating Soil (cont'd.)

Analysis

In which container did the greatest amount of soil move down the mound?

____

____

____

Conclusion

How can you prevent a hill from losing its soil?

____

____

____

© Harcourt Achieve Inc. All rights reserved.

Lesson 8 Objects in the Sky

What do you see when you look up into the sky on a clear night? You may see a beautiful display of stars. A **star** is a glowing ball of gas.

Some stars are brighter than others because they are bigger or hotter. Other stars just seem brighter because they are closer.

Some people use telescopes to look at stars and other objects in the sky. A **telescope** is a tool that makes faraway objects look larger and closer.

Constellations

People have been looking at the stars for a very long time. Long ago, people looked for pictures in groups of stars. They gave names to these groups. A **constellation** is a group of stars that has a name describing the picture it forms.

There are 88 constellations. One constellation looks like a bear. Another looks like a soup ladle. Other constellations look like a lion and a hunter.

star—a glowing ball of gas

telescope—a tool used to see faraway objects in space

constellation—a group of stars that has been given a name based on an imaginary picture it forms

sun—the closest star to Earth

planet—a large object that moves around a star

solar system—the planets and other objects that move around the sun

Constellations

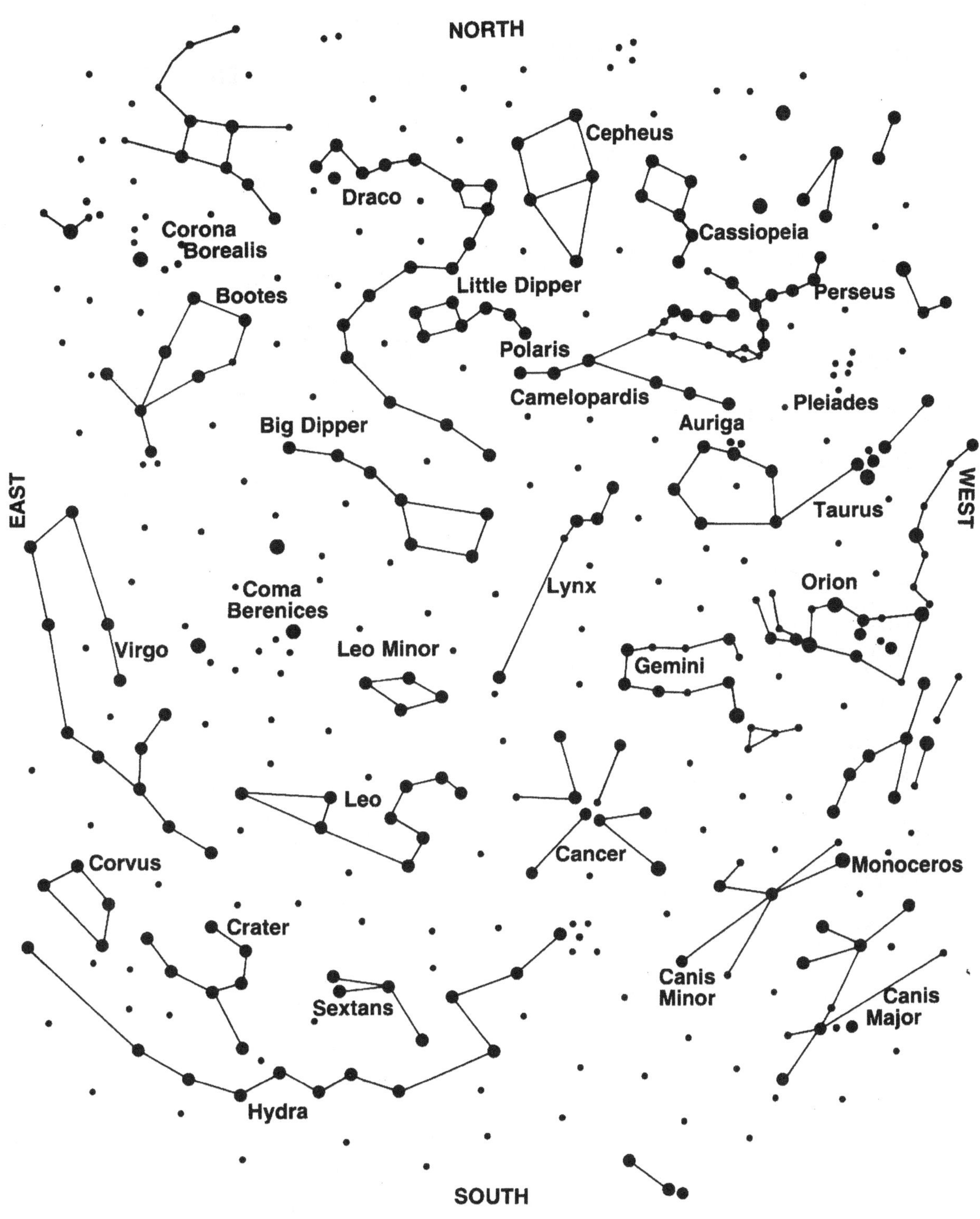

www.harcourtschoolsupply.com
© Harcourt Achieve Inc. All rights reserved.

Lesson 8, Objects in the Sky
Science 2, SV 9781419034305

The Solar System

One very important star is the sun. The **sun** is the closest star to Earth. The sun is huge when compared to Earth. More than one million Earths could fit inside the sun.

When compared with other stars, the sun is average in size. There are many smaller stars and there are many larger stars. The reason the sun looks so large is because the sun is closer to Earth than any other star.

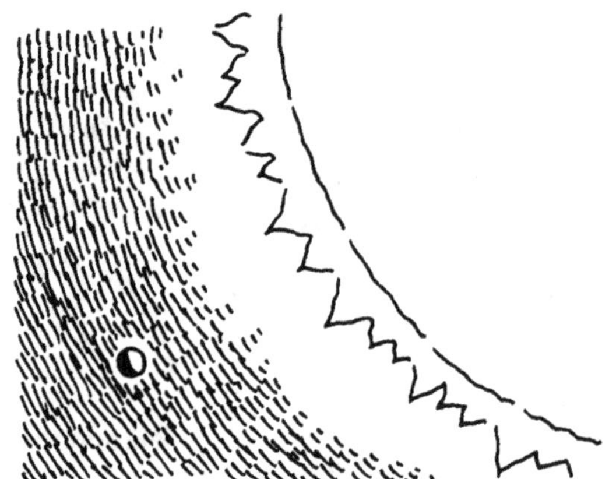

Eight planets move around the sun. A **planet** is a large ball of rock or gas that moves around a star. Earth is one of the planets. The other planets in this solar system are Mercury, Venus, Mars, Jupiter, Saturn, Uranus, and Neptune. The sun and the planets that travel around it make up the **solar system**.

Many of the planets have one or more moons. A moon is an object that moves around a planet. Earth has one moon. Some planets, such as Saturn, have many moons. Other planets, such as Mercury, do not have any moons.

www.harcourtschoolsupply.com
© Harcourt Achieve Inc. All rights reserved.

The Solar System

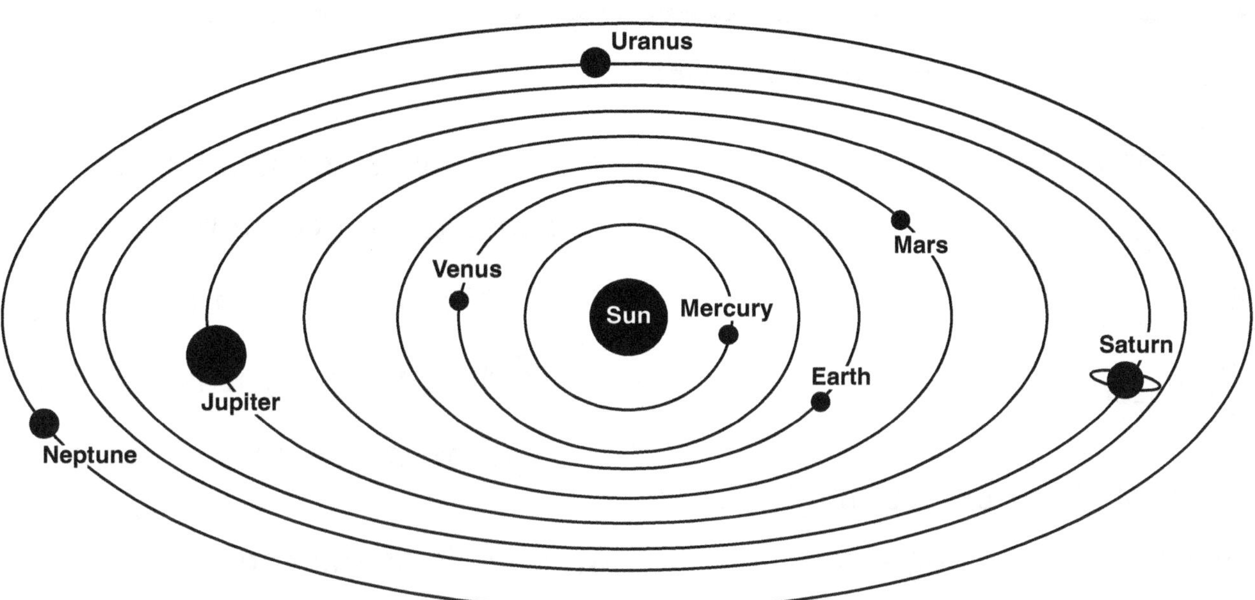

www.harcourtschoolsupply.com
© Harcourt Achieve Inc. All rights reserved.

Lesson 8 Review

Darken the circle by the best answer.

1. A star is made up of

(A) rock.

(B) gas.

(C) water.

2. Which of these objects might someone study using a telescope?

(A) a sample of soil

(B) a plant

(C) a moon

3. Where does the name of a constellation come from?

(A) the picture it forms

(B) how far away it is

(C) how many stars are in it

4. What is at the center of the solar system?

(A) Earth

(B) the moon

(C) the sun

5. Why does the sun look bigger than all other stars?

____

____

____

6. How is a moon different from a planet?

____

____

____

www.harcourtschoolsupply.com
© Harcourt Achieve Inc. All rights reserved.

Lesson 8   The Solar System

Circle the following words in the puzzle below. They may appear horizontally or vertically.

Jupiter	Mars	Mercury
moon	Neptune	planet
Saturn	solar system	star
sun	telescope	Uranus
Venus		

Lesson 8   **The Planets**

Many people make up sentences to remember the order of the planets. This type of sentence is known as a mnemonic (nu-mon-ic). The first letter from each word in the sentence should be the first letter of a planet's name.

Look at the samples shown. Then think of one of your own.

Mercury, **V**enus, **E**arth, **M**ars, **J**upiter, **S**aturn, **U**ranus, **N**eptune

My **V**ery **E**xcellent **M**other **J**ust **S**erved **U**s **N**uts

My **V**ery **E**asy **M**ethod **J**ust **S**imply **U**ses **N**othing

My **V**ery **E**arly **M**orning **J**am **S**andwiches **U**se **N**oodles

M ____

V ____

E ____

M ____

J ____

S ____

U ____

N ____

Lesson 8
Studying the Sky

Write the answer to each of the questions. Choose from the word box below for your answers.

constellation	solar system	sun
moon	star	telescope
planet		

1. What is a glowing ball of gas like our sun? _______________________________

2. What tool can a person use to see the stars? _______________________________

3. What is a group of stars that look like a picture? _______________________________

4. Which star is closest to Earth? _______________________________

5. What is a large object that moves around the sun? _______________________________

6. What are the sun and the eight planets called? _______________________________

7. What type of object moves around Earth? _______________________________

Lesson 8 — Earth's Moon

Read the following passage. Then answer the questions that follow the passage.

The brightest object in the night sky is the moon. People have studied the moon for thousands of years. First they looked at it with their eyes. After the telescope was invented, they were able to see the moon even better.

One of the first people to study the moon carefully was Galileo. He was a scientist who asked questions about the world in the 1600s. Looking through a telescope, he saw that the moon had craters, mountains, and valleys.

Parts of the moon look dark. People once thought that these places were oceans. They named them <u>mare</u>. This comes from the Latin word meaning "seas."

Now people know that there is no liquid water on the moon. Some of the dark places were made by lava a long time ago. Other dark places are formed by shadows. Sometimes

www.harcourtschoolsupply.com
© Harcourt Achieve Inc. All rights reserved.

people think these dark places look like a face on the moon.

Scientists got their first close look at the moon in 1969. That is when an astronaut named Neil Armstrong became the first person to walk on the moon. He and other astronauts collected rocks and pictures from the moon. They also left equipment to study the moon. Scientists have used the information to learn about the inside and outside of the moon.

1. Which sentence about the moon is true?

(A) People did not look at the moon until they had telescopes.

(B) Galileo was the first person to discover the moon.

(C) People studied the moon before the telescope was invented.

2. What is the surface of the moon like?

(A) It is rough like Earth's surface.

(B) It is covered by a huge ocean.

(C) It is very flat and smooth all over.

3. What formed many of the dark areas of the moon?

(A) plants

(B) lava

(C) water

4. How did Neil Armstrong help scientists learn about the moon?

(A) He found oceans on it.

(B) He discovered it for the first time.

(C) He was the first person to go there.

Lesson 8   Experiment: Investigating Constellations

There aren't really pictures in the sky. Constellations are just what people imagine. In this activity, you will make your own constellation.

What You Will Need

sheet of aluminum foil

sharpened pencil

light source

sheet of paper

Procedure

1. With a sharpened pencil point, poke holes in the foil. Be careful not to poke yourself or others when using the pencil.

2. Dim the lights and hold the foil in front of a flashlight or light bulb. The light coming through the holes is like light from a star.

3. Look for a constellation in the stars you made. Draw a picture of your constellation on a sheet of paper.

4. Give your constellation a name. Make up a story to go with it. Show your constellation and tell your story to the class.

Experiment: Investigating Constellations (cont'd.)

Analysis

1. Could you have found more than one constellation among your stars?

____

2. Did you find the same constellations as your classmates?

____

Conclusion

1. What is a constellation?

____

____

____

2. Do you think constellations would be different if they were named today? Why or why not?

____

____

____

Lesson 9 Changes in Earth and Sky

Do you feel like you are moving even when you sit down? You probably don't, but you are actually moving very fast. The reason is that Earth moves.

Day and Night

Earth is shaped like a ball. It spins around like a top. This spinning motion is called **rotation**.

Earth rotates around an imaginary line called an **axis**. You can think of the axis as a line that passes from the North Pole to the South Pole. It takes about 24 hours, or one day, for Earth to spin all the way around.

The sun shines all the time. Only half of Earth faces the sun. As Earth rotates, the part of Earth facing the sun changes.

The part of Earth facing the sun is lit up. It has daytime. The part of Earth facing away from the sun is in darkness. It has nighttime. This is how Earth's rotation causes day and night.

Key Terms

rotation—a spinning motion

axis—an imaginary line around which Earth rotates

orbit—the path of an object around another object

moon—a huge ball of rock that orbits a planet

crater—a large dent on the moon

phases of the moon—the changes in how the moon looks from Earth

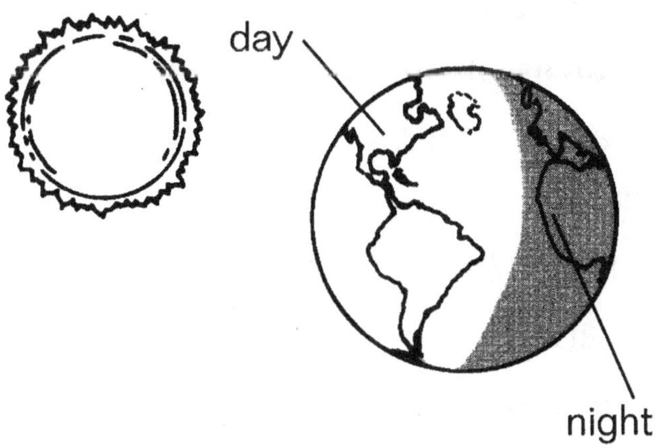

Earth's Orbit

Remember that the planets move around the sun. So as Earth rotates, it also moves around the sun. The path a planet takes around the sun is called an **orbit**. Earth takes one year to orbit the sun.

Earth's axis is tilted. As it orbits the sun, one-half of Earth points toward the sun. The other half of Earth points away from the sun.

The Seasons

When Earth is on one side of the sun, part of Earth points toward the sun. This part of Earth has longer days and higher temperatures. It has summer.

When Earth moves to the other side of the sun, the same part of Earth points away from the sun. Then this part of Earth has shorter days and colder temperatures. It has winter.

There are two points during Earth's orbit when neither part of Earth points toward the sun. These two points mark the beginning of spring and fall.

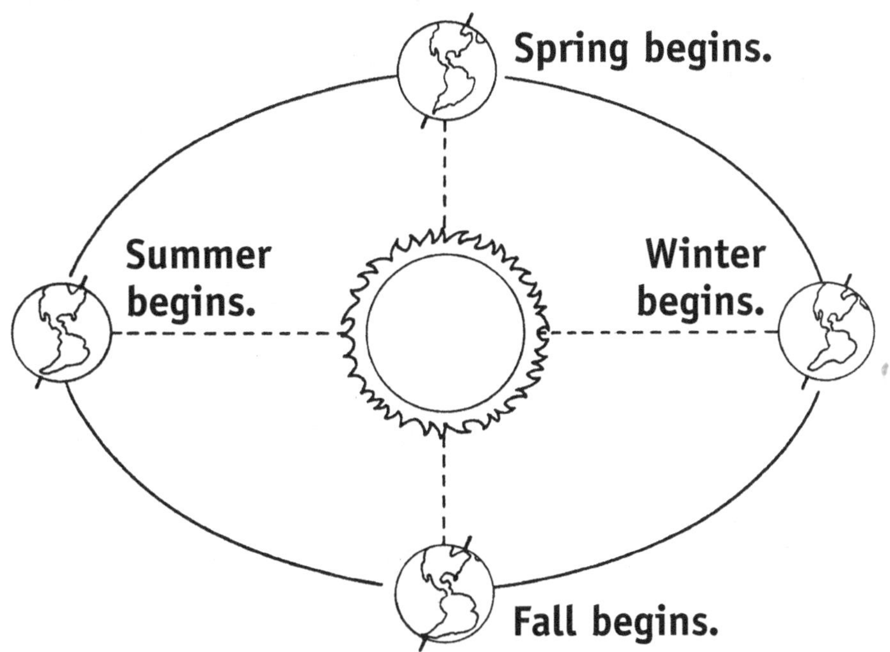

www.harcourtschoolsupply.com
© Harcourt Achieve Inc. All rights reserved.

The Moon

The **moon** is a huge ball of rock that orbits Earth. It takes about 28 days for the moon to orbit Earth. Earth's moon is one of the brightest objects in the night sky. The moon does not make its own light. It is lit up by the sun.

If you look at the moon on a clear night, it might seem to have spots. Many of these spots are large dents called craters. A **crater** forms when a large rock moving through space crashes into the moon.

Phases of the Moon

If you look at the moon at different times the month, it will have different shapes. The moon does not actually change shape. It just looks like it does. The different shapes are known as the **phases of the moon.**

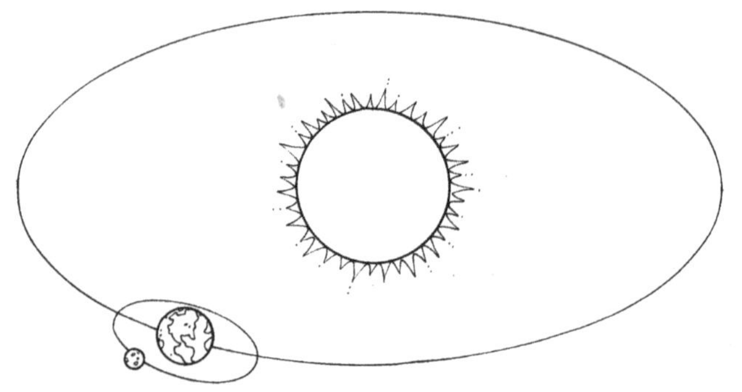

Half of the moon faces the sun. This half is lit up. The other half faces away from the sun. It is dark. As the moon orbits Earth, different amounts of the lit half can be seen from Earth.

Look at the moon in the diagram on page 105. Find the place when the moon is between Earth and the sun. During this phase, known as the new moon, a person on Earth can't see any of the lit half of the moon. The moon looks dark.

Now find the place when Earth is between the moon and the sun. During this phase, known as the full moon, a person on Earth can see all of the lit half of the moon. The moon looks like a bright circle.

Look at how the shape of the moon seems to change as it moves. After the new moon, you can see more and more of the lit half. After the full moon phase, you start to see less and less of the lit half. It takes about four weeks for the moon to pass though all the phases. Then they begin again.

www.harcourtschoolsupply.com
© Harcourt Achieve Inc. All rights reserved.

www.harcourtschoolsupply.com
© Harcourt Achieve Inc. All rights reserved.

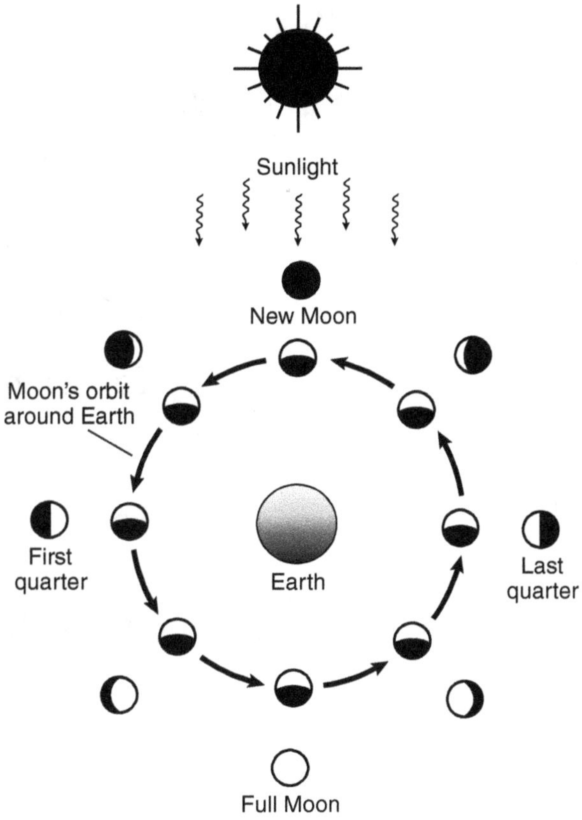

Lesson 9, Changes in Earth and Sky
Science 2, SV 9781419034305

Lesson 9   Review

Darken the circle by the best answer.

1. How long does it take for Earth to complete one rotation?

   (A) one year

   (B) one hour

   (C) one day

2. Earth spins around an imaginary line called the

   (A) rod.

   (B) axis.

   (C) orbit.

3. When Earth completes an orbit, it moves around

   (A) the sun.

   (B) the axis.

   (C) the moon.

4. Which movement causes Earth to have seasons?

   (A) Earth's movement around the sun

   (B) Earth's rotation on its axis

   (C) the moon's movement around Earth

5. Why does the moon have craters?

   (A) The sun burns holes in it.

   (B) Rocks in space crash into it.

   (C) Earth bumps into it.

6. Why does the moon look like it changes shape even when it doesn't?

____

____

____

www.harcourtschoolsupply.com
© Harcourt Achieve Inc. All rights reserved.

Lesson 9

Looking for Changes

Circle the following words in the puzzle below. They may appear horizontally or vertically.

axis	phases	tilt
crater	rotation	winter
day	spring	year
fall	summer	
orbit	sun	

```
X C E O R B I T F A L L
P H A S E S M A B I E O
O C K N S P R I N G B N
H C L A X I S S E J W R
W R N J R T P J Y E I D
H A N S H I D R E A N P
J T E U U L G R A M T S
G E N N G T Q O R N E D
R R O G Y H A T C V R A
G T G R V S U M M E R Y
L W W E Q A Z T K E Z O
E R R O T A T I O N K M
```


www.harcourtschoolsupply.com
© Harcourt Achieve Inc. All rights reserved.

Lesson 9

The Seasons

In most places, the seasons are very different. In the spaces below, draw something related to each season where you live. Try to show how warm or cold it is. Show what a person might wear or do. Show how trees or animals might change.

Spring	Summer
Fall	**Winter**

© Harcourt Achieve Inc. All rights reserved.

Lesson 9   Eclipse

Read the following passage. Then answer the questions that follow the passage.

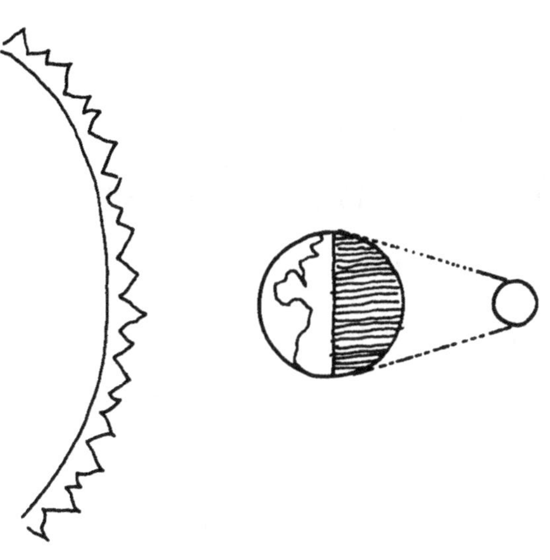

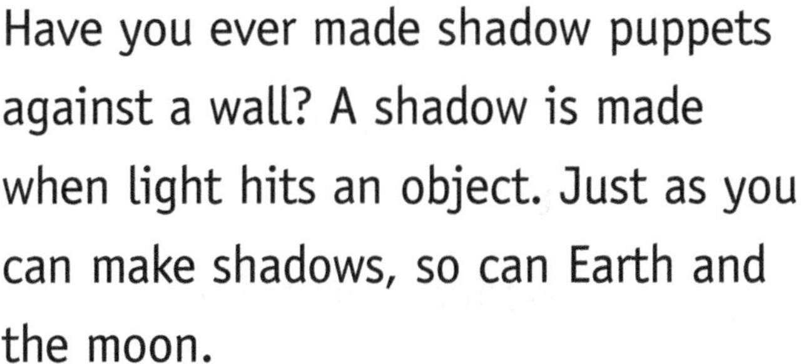

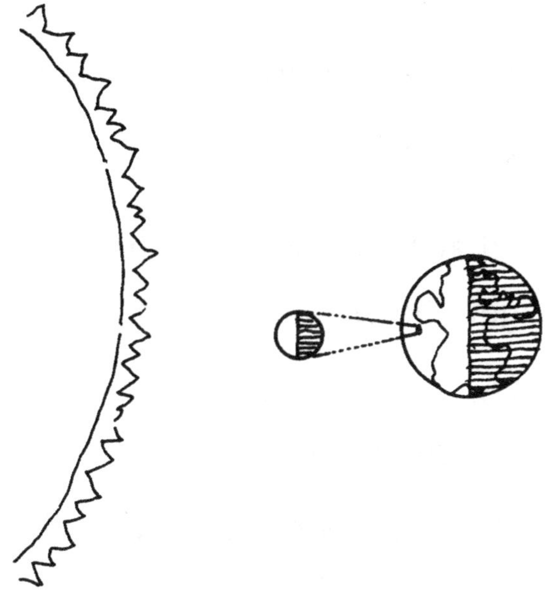

Have you ever made shadow puppets against a wall? A shadow is made when light hits an object. Just as you can make shadows, so can Earth and the moon.

The moon moves around Earth. Sometimes the moon gets between the sun and Earth. Some of the light from the sun cannot reach Earth. Instead, it hits the moon. This makes a shadow on Earth. This is known as a solar eclipse. The word <u>solar</u> describes things involving the sun.

A different type of shadow forms when the moon moves all the way around to the other side of Earth. This time Earth is between the moon and the sun. Some of the light from the sun is blocked by Earth. A lunar eclipse happens when the moon moves into the shadow that Earth makes. The word <u>lunar</u> describes things involving the moon.

1. What causes a shadow to form?

(A) A light goes out.

(B) Light is blocked by an object.

(C) Light passes through an object.

2. What happens when the moon gets between Earth and the sun?

(A) The sun makes a shadow on the moon.

(B) The moon makes a shadow on Earth.

(C) Earth makes a shadow on the sun.

3. How are the moon, sun, and Earth arranged during a lunar eclipse?

(A) The moon is between Earth and the sun.

(B) The sun is between Earth and the moon.

(C) Earth is between the moon and the sun.

4. When is the word <u>lunar</u> used?

(A) to describe something about the moon

(B) to describe something about the sun

(C) to describe something about Earth

Lesson 9 — Experiment: Investigating Day and Night

Each day on Earth lasts about 24 hours. What causes day and night? What determines the length of day and night?

What You Will Need

balloon
flashlight
marker
paper

Procedure

1. Use a marker to draw a person on the inflated balloon.

2. Dim the lights and have a partner shine the flashlight on the balloon.

3. Draw a picture on the paper showing what part of the balloon is lit up.

4. Slowly rotate the balloon and watch your person move. Draw a diagram comparing the motion of the person to the part of the balloon that is lit up.

5. Spin the balloon so that it rotates faster. Then make it rotate more slowly. Watch how the motion of the person changes.

Analysis

1. What part of the balloon had daytime?

____

____

Experiment: Investigating Day and Night (cont'd.)

2. What part of the balloon had night?

____

____

3. Why did the person on the balloon have both day and night each day?

____

____

Conclusion

How would the length of each day on Earth change if Earth rotated faster or more slowly?

____

____

____

Science Fair Projects

You may want to know about nature. You might do a project to learn.

A science fair project is a science activity. It has many parts to it. A science fair project will take longer than one class period.

Choose a Topic

Start by picking what you want to learn about. You might pick animals or plants. You might pick rocks. You might even pick weather. Whatever you decide to study is your topic.

Then ask a question about your topic. You might ask how rocks can be different. You might ask what clouds tell about weather.

Find Information

You need to learn about your topic. You can look in books or magazines. You might also use the Internet.

You can talk to people who know about the topic. You might ask a gardener about plants. You might ask a doctor about your heartbeat.

www.harcourtschoolsupply.com
© Harcourt Achieve Inc. All rights reserved.

Types of Projects

There are three basic types of projects.

An Experiment An experiment is a test. The test will answer your question.

You begin by making a guess. Then you test your guess.

Suppose you want to know if plant food helps plants grow. You guess that it does.

Then you grow two plants. You add plant food to only one.

You look at the plants every day. You write down how each one looks. You measure each plant.

You think about what happened. You try to figure out what it means. You might decide that plant food did help one plant grow.

Was your guess right? Sometimes your guess is right. Sometimes it is not. Either way, you learn something from your experiment.

An Exhibit Some science projects are not experiments. Some are models of things in nature. They show what things look like.

Other science projects are demonstrations. They show how things happen in nature.

An exhibit should teach something. You might show how a volcano erupts.

A Collection For this type of project, you collect things. The things should be from nature. You might collect rocks or leaves.

You put the things into groups. The things in each group should be the same. You might group rocks by their color. You might group leaves by their shape.

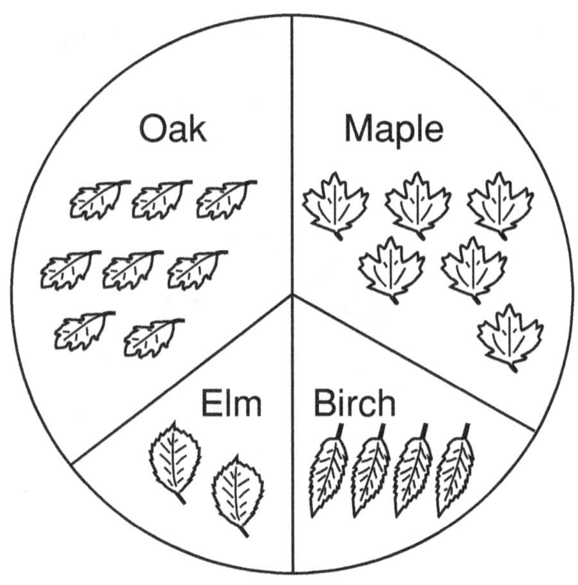

www.harcourtschoolsupply.com
© Harcourt Achieve Inc. All rights reserved.

Science Fair Projects
Science 2, SV 9781419034305

Safety

It is important to stay safe during a project. Always listen to your teacher or parent.

Check with your teacher or parent before starting a project. Ask your teacher or parent if you are not sure something is safe. Let your teacher or parent know if something breaks or spills.

While working on your project, follow these safety tips. Wear safety goggles. Tie back long hair. Do not wear loose clothing. Never eat or drink anything unless your teacher or parent tells you to.

Project Notebook

Write down everything about your project. Keep your notes in a notebook. You should include these pages.

Title Page Write the title of your project. Print your name and teacher's name. Write the date.

Table of Contents List what is in your report. Give the page number of each part of the report.

Overview Tell why you did the project. Write a few sentences telling what you did. Tell what you learned.

Materials List the things you used. Tell the sizes of items and how many you used.

Experiment and Data Write the steps you followed. Show any drawings you made. Paste any photos you took. Write what you did and saw. Make graphs and charts of your data when you can.

Conclusion Tell what you found out. Tell if your guess was right.

Sources List where you got information. List the names of the books, magazines, or newspapers. List the names of the people you asked.

www.harcourtschoolsupply.com
© Harcourt Achieve Inc. All rights reserved.

Presenting the Project

You need to show what you learned. You should show your science notebook. You should make a display. The display should be neat and easy to follow.

Your display should tell about your project. It should show any pictures, graphs, or charts you made. Show any things you collected.

Project Ideas

There are many great ideas for a science fair project. On pages 117–118 is a list of some questions you can think about.

You might use one of them. You might get your own idea from looking at these.

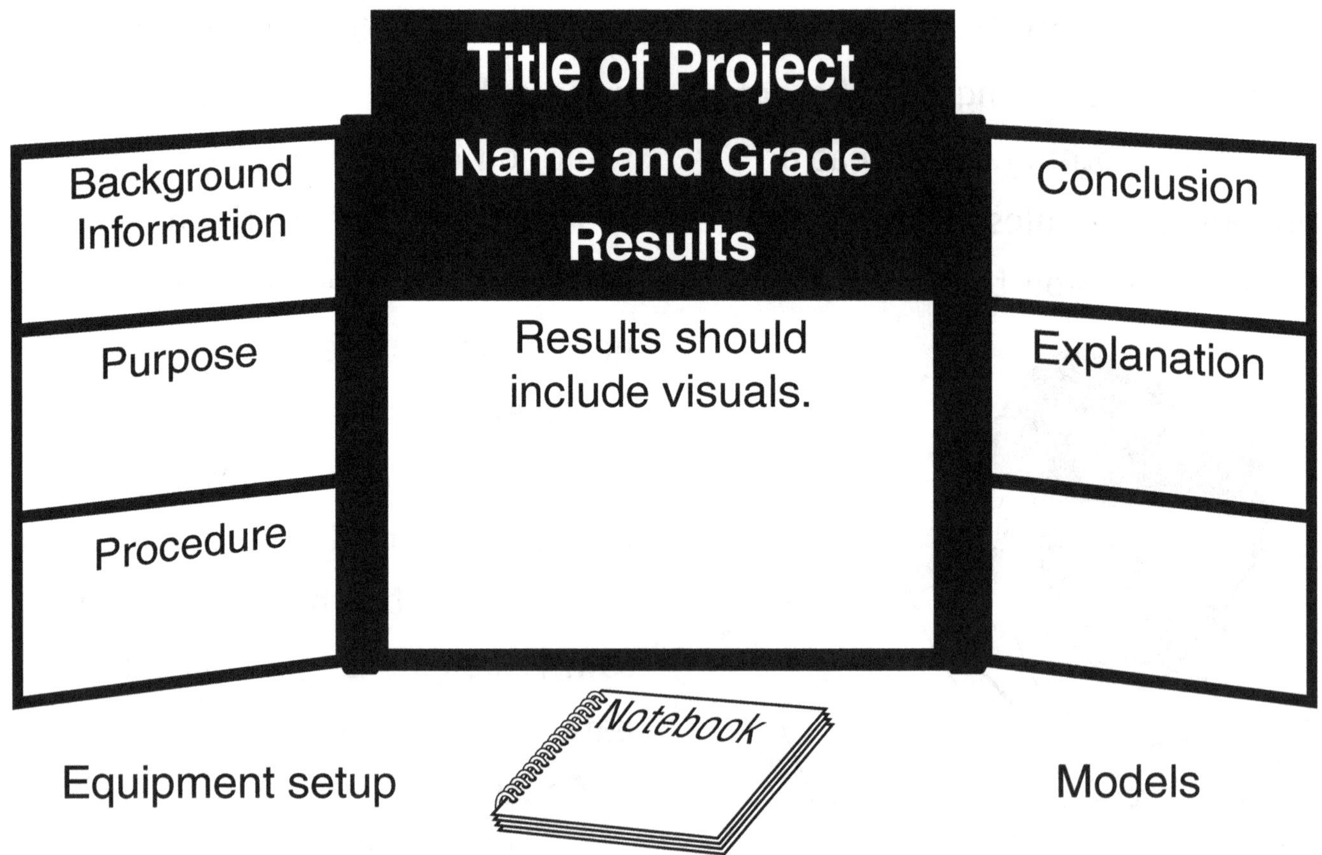

www.harcourtschoolsupply.com
© Harcourt Achieve Inc. All rights reserved.

Science Fair Projects
Science 2, SV 9781419034305

- **How can objects have the same size but different masses?** Compare several objects by mass and size.

- **Can you add salt to water to make an egg float?** Add different amounts of salt to water in clear containers. Find out if a hard-boiled egg can float in each one.

- **What is the water cycle?** Show how water changes state and how this makes rain and snow.

- **How can a map show a change in position?** Make a map. Compare how far an object moves through the streets of the map with the total distance it moves from its original place.

- **How fast can you move?** Measure and compare your speed when you walk, run, and bike some distance.

- **How much iron is in different cereals?** Use a strong magnet to compare cereals.

- **How can colors combine to make white light?** Show how different colors of light combine. Use paint colors to compare.

- **How does the sun heat sand?** Place containers of sand in the sun and in the shade. Compare the starting and ending temperatures of the sand in each container.

- **How do different fertilizers affect plant growth?** Add different brands of fertilizer to plants. Find out if some plants grow better than others.

- **How does salt water affect plant growth?** Water one group of plants with regular water. Water another group with salt water. Find out if one group of plants grows better than the other.

- **Which types of plants are better at surviving a drought?** Grow several different types of plants or get seedlings for them. Once the plants are about the same age, stop watering them or give them only a little water. Find out which type of plants survives and stays the healthiest.

© Harcourt Achieve Inc. All rights reserved.

- **What are the food groups that a person needs to eat?** Show samples of foods from different groups. Tell what materials people get from each food group.

- **How do different conditions affect how fast a seed becomes a seedling?** Plant seeds in several different containers. Change the conditions for the plants. For example, give one lots of water and another very little. Place one in direct sunlight and another in shade. Find out which seed sprouts the fastest.

- **How old are trees?** Show how tree rings can be used to find the age of a tree. Tell what other information tree rings can give about the tree.

- **What is inside a fruit?** Fruits have seeds in them. Show examples of different fruits and their seeds. Describe what else is in a fruit. Tell how fruits help the plant to make more plants.

- **Do plants grow better in natural light or artificial light?** Grow some plants in sunlight and others under indoor lights. Try different kinds of indoor lighting. Find out which plants grow better.

- **What lives in a habitat?** Choose and explore a habitat. Show what plants and animals live in it and where it is.

- **What are the properties of different rocks?** Collect rocks and list their properties. Classify them into groups.

- **How do crystals form?** Make rock candy to show how crystals form.

- **How is the solar system arranged?** Make a model of the solar system.

- **How do constellations change during the year?** Show how the constellations you can see change during the year because of Earth's motion.

Glossary

axis—an imaginary line around which Earth rotates (p. 102)

balance—a tool that measures mass (p. 7)

cell—the basic unit of life (p. 45)

charge—an electrical force that can be either positive (+) or negative (−) (p.32)

circuit—a path through which electric current can flow (p. 32)

constellation—a group of stars that has been given a name based on an imaginary picture it forms (p. 90)

crater—a large dent on the moon (p. 102)

desert—an environment that does not get much rain (p. 66)

distance—the length an object moves (p. 20)

egg—the first stage in the life cycle of many living things (p. 56)

electric current—the flow of electric charge (p. 32)

energy—the ability to cause change (p. 32)

environment—the living and nonliving things in a place (p. 66)

food chain—a diagram that shows how energy moves from plants to animals (p. 66)

forest—an environment that gets enough rain for many trees to grow (p. 66)

gas—matter that does not have a certain size or shape (p. 7)

habitat—a place where an organism finds the things it needs to live (p. 66)

heat—the flow of thermal energy from a warmer object to a cooler one (p. 32)

life cycle—the changes that occur to a living thing between birth and death (p. 56)

liquid—matter that has a certain size but takes the shape of its container (p. 7)

living—something that is alive, and grows and changes (p. 45)

magnet—an object that can push or pull some types of matter (p. 32)

mass—the amount of matter in an object (p. 7)

matter—anything that has mass and takes up space (p. 7)

moon—a huge ball of rock that orbits a planet (p. 102)

www.harcourtschoolsupply.com
© Harcourt Achieve Inc. All rights reserved.

motion—a change in the position of an object (p. 20)

natural resource—something that people can use that is found in nature (p. 81)

nonliving—something that is not alive, and does not grow and change (p. 45)

ocean—a large body of salt water (p. 66)

orbit—the path of an object around another object (p. 102)

phases of the moon—the changes in how the moon looks from Earth (p. 102)

planet—a large object that moves around a star (p. 90)

pole—a region of a magnet where the magnetic effects are strongest (p. 32)

pond—a freshwater environment (p. 66)

position—the location of an object (p. 20)

property—a trait that can describe matter (p. 7)

rain forest—a warm environment that gets rain all year long (p. 66)

ray—a straight path of light (p. 32)

resource—anything people can use (p. 81)

rock—a hard, nonliving thing that comes from Earth (p. 81)

rotation—a spinning motion (p. 102)

seed—the first stage in the life cycle of many plants (p. 56)

solar system—the planets and other objects that move around the sun (p. 90)

solid—matter that has a certain shape and size (p. 7)

speed—how fast or slowly an object moves (p. 20)

star—a glowing ball of gas (p. 90)

sun—the closest star to Earth (p. 90)

telescope—a tool used to see faraway objects in space (p. 90)

texture—the way a sample of matter feels (p. 7)

transportation—a way that people move things from one place to another (p. 81)

tundra—a cold, dry environment (p. 66)

volume—the amount of space an object takes up (p. 7)

www.harcourtschoolsupply.com
© Harcourt Achieve Inc. All rights reserved.

Answer Key

Assessment, pp. 5-6
1. A	**2.** C	**3.** B	**4.** C
5. C	**6.** B	**7.** B	**8.** A
9. B	**10.** C	**11.** B	**12.** C
13. C	**14.** A	**15.** B	**16.** C
17. C	**18.** B		

Unit 1 Lesson 1
Review, p. 12

1. C	**2.** C	**3.** B
4. A	**5.** B	**6.** C

7. All types of matter have mass and take up space.

All About Matter, p. 13
Students should circle the terms in the word search.

Solids, Liquids, and Gases, p. 14
1. matter	**2.** texture
3. solid	**4.** mass
5. property	**6.** balance
7. liquid	**8.** volume
9. gas	

States of Matter, p. 15
1. liquid	**2.** solid
3. solid	**4.** gas
5. liquid	

Properties of Matter, p. 16
Answers will vary. Check that the properties students write match the matter.

Changing States of Water, p. 17
Students should show ice changing into liquid water changing into water vapor. Encourage them to show how heat is involved in the changes.

Experiment: Investigating the Mass of a Gas, p. 19
Analysis

1. I balanced the straw to show that it was balanced before the balloons were added to it. This way I would know that any changes would be because of the balloons.
2. No, the straw with the filled balloon was much lower than the straw with the empty balloon.

Conclusion

Air must have mass. The two balloons were the same before I blew one up. The only

www.harcourtschoolsupply.com
© Harcourt Achieve Inc. All rights reserved.

Answer Key
Science 2, SV 9781419034305

difference was the air I added to it. The air made the filled balloon have more mass than the empty balloon.

Unit 1 Lesson 2
Review, p. 23
1. B   2. A   3. C   4. B
5. It is changing position, or location.
6. The speed tells the amount of time it takes for an object to move a certain distance.

Position, p. 24
Check student descriptions for accuracy.

Showing Motion, p. 25
Students should show that an object changed position.

Distance, p. 26
1. 9 centimeters
2. 4 centimeters
3. 12 centimeters
4. 7 centimeters

Speed, p. 27
snail = 1
baby = 2
bicycle = 3
train = 4
airplane = 5

The Crawler, p. 29
1. A   2. B   3. C   4. C   5. B

Experiment: Investigating Motion, p. 31
Analysis
The person who took giant steps reached the end first.
Conclusion
1. The person who took giant steps walked faster.
2. The person had a faster speed because he or she moved a greater distance in the same amount of time.
3. If both people moved the same distance in the same amount of time, they would move at the same speed. They would both reach the end at the same time.

Unit 1 Lesson 3
Review, p. 36
1. A   2. C   3. A   4. B   5. A
6. Heat will flow from the spoon to the sink. It flows from a warmer object to a cooler one.

Light, p. 37
1. all
2. some
3. some
4. none
5. Accept answers based on the following: milk = none; glass = all; carton = none.
6. all
7. all
8. all
9. none

Answer Key cont'd.

Movement of Light, p. 38

A Students should show an arrow coming back from the mirror. The angle is not important at this point. Instead, it is important for students to identify reflection.

B Students should show an arrow moving through the window. It would be good if students show the light bending. However, the angle is not important at this point. Instead, it is important for students to identify that the light passes through the window.

Heat Flow, p. 39

1. from water to ice
2. from stove to pot
3. from carrot to snowman
4. from toast to plate

Heat Change, p. 40

1. Students color the toasted bread.
2. Students color the popped corn.
3. Students color the cooked eggs.
4. Students color the glass of water.

Types of Energy, p. 41

ray → light
charge → electrical force
magnet → pole
heat → thermal energy
current → circuit

Check students' sentences.

A Compass, p. 42

1. A   2. C   3. A   4. B

Experiment: Investigating Light, p. 44

Analysis

1. Yes, it did.
2. No, it did not.

Conclusion

Light travels in a straight line as long as it stays in one type of matter, such as air.

Unit 2 Lesson 4

Review, p. 48

1. C   2. A   3. C   4. B   5. A   6. B
7. It is made of cells, it reacts to its environment, and it can make more bean plants.

Living and Nonliving Things, p. 49

1. N   2. L   3. L   10. L
4. N   5. L   6. L
7. N   8. N   9. N

Living Things, p. 50

Answers may vary.

1. cells
2. makes more living things
3. needs energy
4. needs water
5. grows and changes
6. reacts

Living Things Around Me, p. 51

Students should show animals, plants, and people on the left side of the chart. They should include nonliving items such as furniture, toys, and appliances on the right side of the chart. Encourage students to be creative. They might extend the activity to

www.harcourtschoolsupply.com
© Harcourt Achieve Inc. All rights reserved.

Answer Key
Science 2, SV 9781419034305

Answer Key cont'd.

make a chart for different rooms. They might make a chart for inside and outside. Students might find photos of items in magazines or newspapers, or they might even take their own photos.

Coral Reefs, p. 53
1. C   **2.** B   **3.** A   **4.** C   **5.** A

Experiment: Looking at Living Things, p. 55
Analysis
Answers may vary, but students should observe that the living thing eats, reacts, and breathes. Encourage students to describe specific examples.
Conclusion
Living things have the same basic characteristics. Allow students to compare results to find that different kinds of living things have these same characteristics.

Unit 2 Lesson 5
Review, p. 59
1. C   **2.** B   **3.** A   **4.** C   **5.** B
6. All mammals drink milk from their mothers.

Growing Up, p. 60
Students should write about three sentences. They should describe something about how the baby lion drank milk from its mother. The lion cub was bigger and moved faster. The grown lion could take care of itself. It looked like its parents. Accept any answers that show that students recognize how the lion grew and changed.

Butterfly Life Cycle, p. 61
1. egg
2. caterpillar
3. cocoon
4. butterfly

Seeds, p. 62
Students should describe each type of seed. If the seeds were purchased in packets, students might tape a photo of the seed or the plant onto the chart. Encourage students to drop some seeds to see if they are carried by wind.

Seeds We Eat, p. 63
Students should circle the popcorn, peanuts, peanut butter, wheat (bread), peas, and beans.

Experiment: Investigating the Life Cycle of a Plant, p. 65
Analysis
The seeds came from a plant that was already grown.
Conclusion
The life cycle of a plant includes changing from a seed, to a seedling, to a full-grown plant. The plant then makes seeds that can make more plants.

Unit 2 Lesson 6
Review, p. 71
1. A   **2.** C   **3.** B   **4.** C   **5.** A   **6.** B
7. They have thick fat and fur to keep them warm.

www.harcourtschoolsupply.com
© Harcourt Achieve Inc. All rights reserved.

Answer Key
Science 2, SV 9781419034305

Answer Key cont'd.

Wet or Dry?, p. 72
1. dry
2. wet

Where Things Live, p. 74
Across
2. forest
4. ocean
8. environment
10. tundra
Down
1. blubber
3. sunlight
5. cactus
6. desert
7. food
9. pond

Different Habitats, p. 75
1. tundra
2. forest
3. rain forest
4. desert
5. ocean
6. pond

Ant Habitat, p. 76
1. 6
2. 25

Ocean Food Chain, p. 77
Picture order: 2, 3, 1, 4
1. They would die.
2. They would die
3. No, there would not be any fish.
4. All living things depend on plants because they eat the plants or they eat animals that eat the plants.

The Arctic Hare, p. 78
1. the tundra
2. white
3. gray and brown
4. The colors of the arctic hare help it blend into the color of the ground.

Experiment: Investigating Environments, p. 80
Analysis
Students should find that a greater number of white circles are picked up.
Conclusions
1. The black circles were harder to see than the white circles.
2. If white paper was used, more black circles would be picked up than white circles.
3. Living things that are the same color as their background are harder to see. This helps living things stay safe.

Unit 3 Lesson 7
Review, p. 83
1. C   2. A   3. B   4. A   5. B
6. People use rock to build roads, make buildings, and create sculptures.

Earth's Materials, p. 84
1. rock
2. transportation
3. resource
4. soil
5. water

Check students' sentences.

www.harcourtschoolsupply.com
© Harcourt Achieve Inc. All rights reserved.

Answer Key
Science 2, SV 9781419034305

Resources on Earth, p. 85

1. natural
2. rock
3. roads
4. soil
5. adobe
6. water
7. transportation
8. electricity

Mt. Rushmore, p. 87

1. B   2. A   3. C   4. B

Experiment: Investigating Soil, p. 89

Analysis

The greatest amount of soil moved in container 1.

Conclusion

The loss of soil can be slowed by preventing water from flowing straight down the hill. Something in the way of the water slows it down. Circles on the hill also slow the flow of water.

Unit 3 Lesson 8

Review, p. 94

1. B   2. C   3. A   4. C
5. The sun is closer to Earth than all the other stars. This makes the sun look bigger.
6. A moon moves around a planet. A planet moves around the sun.

The Solar System, p. 95

Check to see that students have circled every term.

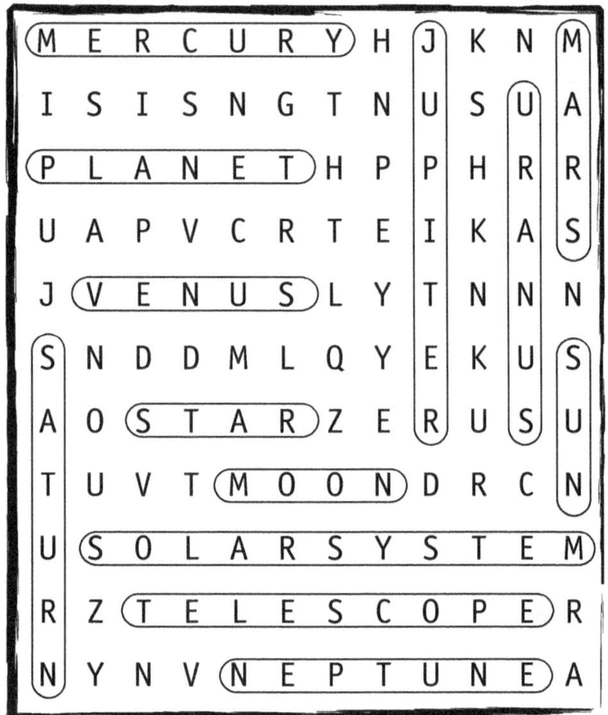

The Planets, p. 96

Check that student sentences use each of the eight letters. The sentences do not have to make sense and can be silly or creative.

Studying the Sky, p. 97

1. star
2. telescope
3. constellation
4. sun
5. planet
6. solar system
7. moon

www.harcourtschoolsupply.com
© Harcourt Achieve Inc. All rights reserved.

Answer Key
Science 2, SV 9781419034305

Answer Key cont'd.

Earth's Moon, p. 99
1. C **2.** A **3.** B **4.** C

Experiment: Investigating Constellations, p. 101
Analysis
1. Students should be able to find more than one constellation if they use their imaginations.
2. Every person should most likely find a different picture.

Conclusion
1. A constellation is a picture found by connecting stars like dots. It is based on a person's imagination and stories he or she may know.
2. Constellations probably would have different names because people know different stories and characters today.

Unit 3 Lesson 9
Review, p. 106
1. C
2. B
3. A
4. A
5. B
6. Half of the moon is always lit by the sun. As the moon moves around Earth, people on Earth can see different parts of the lit side.

Looking for Changes, p. 107

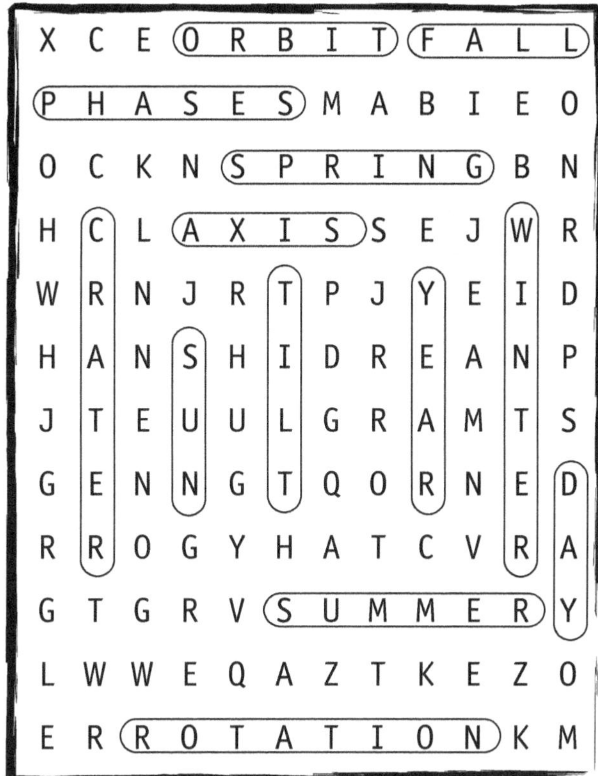

The Seasons, p. 108
Students should draw pictures related to each season. For example, they might draw flowers blooming in spring and leaves dropping from trees in fall.

Eclipse, p. 110
1. B
2. B
3. C
4. A

www.harcourtschoolsupply.com
© Harcourt Achieve Inc. All rights reserved.

Answer Key cont'd.

Experiment: Investigating Day and Night, pp. 111–112

Analysis

1. The part lit by the flashlight had daytime.
2. The dark part had night.
3. As Earth rotated, the person moved through the lit part and the dark part.

Conclusion

The length of each day depends on how fast Earth rotates. If it rotated faster, one day would be shorter. If it rotated more slowly, one day would last longer.

© Harcourt Achieve Inc. All rights reserved.

www.ingramcontent.com/pod-product-compliance
Lightning Source LLC
Chambersburg PA
CBHW081506120326
41115CB00007B/97